Grades 2-6
Multi-Curricular

Springboards & Starters

Written by
Linda Milliken

Illustrated by
Barb Lorseyedi

Cover Design
Wendy Loreen

Cover Illustration
Priscilla Burris

ISBN 1-56472-010-1

Multicurricular Springboards and Starters © 1993

Edupress • PO Box 883 • Dana Point CA 92629

Table of Contents

Talk About Topics

Discussion leads to discovery, better communication skills. and a more positive self-image. Develop oral language skills with a variety of approaches.

Thinking Skills

Challenge students to develop higher levels of thinking with these "thought provoking" starters –for writing and discussion.

Creative Investigations

Expand student's base of information literacy by providing a host of subjects to explore and research.

Table of Contents

Literature and Writing Sparks

*Fresh ideas to get writing off the ground and extend
literature encounters ... creatively.*

Cooperative Experiences

*Innovative ways to mix students and learning. Here is a variety of
formats and subjects for promoting group involvement.*

Subject Stimulation

*Core-curriculum can be interesting, thought-provoking, integrated and varied.
Here are prompts offered by subject.*

Table of Contents

Pleasurable Pursuits

Themes and studies with something for everyone to make school days exciting and extend core curriculum.

Seatwork Jump Start

Need a reproducible with meaningful learning in a hurry? Here are some pages for just that purpose.

Bulletin Board Boosts

Easy ways to turn walls, doors and bulletin boards into appealing, interactive learning opportunities.

Table of Contents

Inventive Incentive

Awards, charts, coupons and inventive ways to recognize, motivate and reward students.

Say it in a SONG

Song lyrics provide the basis for some meaningful discussion about feelings, friendship and attitude.

Start with these old "standards." If you don't know the melody, pick up some albums at the library or ask parents and grandparents to come in and lead a song fest in your classroom.

THE BEST THINGS IN LIFE ARE FREE

The moon belongs to everyone,
The best things in life are free.
The stars belong to everyone,
They gleam there for you and me.
The flowers in spring,
The robins that sing,
The sunbeams that shine,
They're yours, they're mine.
And love can come to everyone,
The best things in life are free.

Discussion:
  Different kinds of wealth; appreciation;
  enjoyment; love

SIDE BY SIDE

Oh, we ain't got a barrel of money.
Maybe we're ragged and funny, but
We'll travel along, singing a song.
Side by side.
We don't know what's coming tomorrow.
Maybe it's trouble and sorrow, but
We'll travel the road, sharing our load,
Side by Side.
In all kinds of weather, what if the sky should fall.
As long as we're together, it doesn't matter at all.
We've all had our troubles and parted.
We'll be the same as we started.
Just travelin' along, singin' a song.
Side by side.

Discussion:
  friendship, teamwork, fidelity, hope,
  facing problems

ME AND MY SHADOW

Me and my shadow, strolling down the avenue.
Me and my shadow, not a soul to tell our troubles to.
And when it's twelve o'clock,
We climb the stairs,we never knock
For nobody's there.
Just me and my shadow,
All alone and feeling blue.

Discussion:
Loneliness; sadness; making friends

WHEN YOU'RE SMILING

When you're smiling, when you're smiling,
The whole world smiles with you.
When you're laughing, when you're laughing,
The sun comes shiinng through.
But when you're crying, you bring on the rain,
So stop your sighing, be happy again.
Keep on smiling, 'cause when you're smiling,
The whole world smiles with you.

Discussion:
Mental outlook, expressing feelings, pouting

Say it
in a
SONG

APRIL SHOWERS

Though April showers may come your way,
They bring the flowers that bloom in May.
So if it's raining, have no regrets
Because it isn't raining rain, you know,
It's raining violets;
And when you see clouds upon the hills,
You soon will see crowds of daffodil,
So keep on looking for a bluebird
And listening for his song,
Whenever April showers come along.

Discussion:
Positive thinking, optimism, disappointment

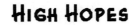

HIGH HOPES

Once there was a silly ol' ant,
Thought he'd move a rubber tree plant.
Anyone knows an ant, can't,
Mover a rubber tree plant—but
He had high hopes, he had high hopes
He had high apple pie in the sky hopes.
So any time you're feeling low,
'Stead of letting go,
Just remember that ant.
Whoops, there goes another rubber tree,
Whoops, there goes another rubber tree plant—KERPLOP!

Discussion:
Effort, persistence, hope

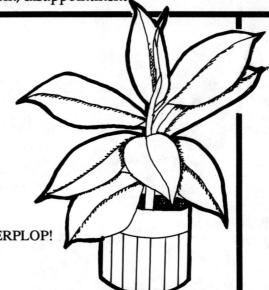

A HOST OF HOW-TOS

Use these directives to see how well your students can verbally describe simple "how-tos". Try some where students cannot use any props and try others where students can use simple props in addition to words.

☞ How to make a chicken salad sandwich on white toast

☞ How to make a bunk bed

☞ How to put fresh florist-delivered flowers into a vase

☞ How to pack for a weekend of skiing using one suitcase

☞ How to bake chocolate chip cookies

☞ How to prepare hot dogs on buns for a group of six

☞ How to make fresh-squeezed orange juice

☞ How to bag groceries at the supermarket

☞ How to make a (choose your own flavor) ice cream soda

☞ How to gift wrap a large teddy bear

☞ How to play checkers

☞ How to catch a butterfly

☞ How to help a baby learn to walk

☞ How to play the card game 'Go Fish'

☞ How to make pancakes

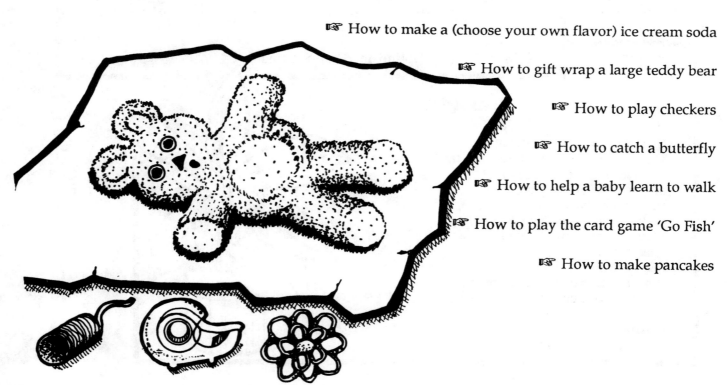

SILLY STUFF
to talk about

Sometimes we all need a light-hearted moment or two to unwind. Use these topics to add a few minutes of humor in the classroom and promote communication skills at the same time.

A Silly YOU

You've won a contest and can have dinner with a celebrity of your choice. Who will you choose? Why?

There's a new television sitcom based on your life. What would the show be called? What would some of the shows be about?

If you had the choice of being rich or famous or beautiful (handsome), which would you choose?

If you could have a special power over people, what power would you like to have? How would you use it?

Imagine that you could have a free, lifetime supply of any product or food that you want. What would you choose? (It can't be money!)

If you could change one thing about your appearance, what would you change?

A Silly WORLD

What would you like to see disappear from your house? your school? the world?

Where do you think would be the silliest place in the world to visit?

Look up names of villages, towns and cities in the atlas and talk about all the ones with funny or silly names.

If you could make one sport the official "world sport", which one would you choose?

Who is the silliest person you ever heard about?

► Delve Into Debates

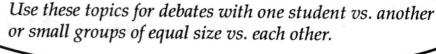

Use these topics for debates with one student vs. another or small groups of equal size vs. each other.

➤ Student groups should be allowed to decide on curriculum and school policy.

➤ To protect the environment and prevent oil spills, the importation of oil on large barges should be prohibited.

➤ Every school should be on a year-round cycle.

➤ The government should grant a free college education to students who have always maintained outstanding grades.

➤ To protect the lives of fur-bearing animals, people should not be allowed to wear fur coats.

➤ The government should provide national health insurance that gives the same protection to all citizens.

➤ All communities should enforce separating trash items.

➤ The main purpose of animals is to serve the needs of humans.

➤ No one should be allowed to own a gun.

➤ All restaurants must have a non-smoking section.

➤ Airports that are close to residential communities should ban takeoffs and landings between 11 0'clock in the evening and 7 o'clock in the morning.

➤ People should not waste water even when there are no drought conditions.

➤ There should be one unit of currency for the entire world.

➤ The government should establish a list of ecology guidelines, which if followed, would allow citizens a tax deduction.

➤ People over the age of 21 should volunteer at least two hours weekly to community service.

Multicurricular SPRINGBOARDS & STARTERS © EDUPRESS

Quick
Tricks for Talking

Sometimes just getting the courage to speak in front of a group is half the battle. Here are some simple prompts that might make that "speaking experience" a little bit easier to face.

Start with a ball of string and a pair of scissors. Ask each student to cut a length—any length—of string and pass the ball and scissors to the next person. When everyone has a piece of string, announce a topic. Each child must speak about the topic while winding the string around his or her finger. When the string is completely wound, their talking turn is over.

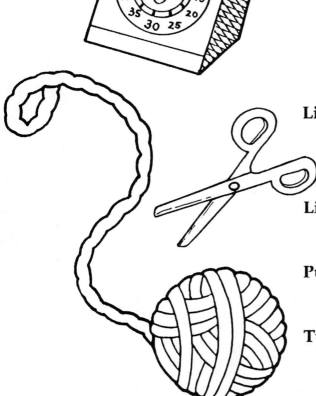

While sitting in a circle, try these two talk tricks:

• Toss a foam ball to a student. He or she speaks about a selected topic for 30 seconds then tosses the ball to someone else in the circle.

• Pass out slips of paper, numbered with as many numbers as there are students in the circle. Pass out the number slips to each student in the circle. Students speak about a selected topic in the order of the number each holds.

Limit the talk time. Use a selection of timers to bring talks to an end. Try a sand timer from a board game. Use a standard kitchen timer but preselect the number of minutes a person will speak. Children may find there's more to say than they thought.

Limit the talk quantity. Inform students they are to say only two sentences about a talk topic. Hold to that limit; then move on to the next speaker.

Put the spotlight on the speaker—literally. Hav a flashlight handy. Shine the flashlight on the face of the speaker.

Turn out the lights. Tap the shoulder of the child who is to speak next on a given topic. Students may feel more comfortable speaking anonymously in the dark.

PICK A LETTER

Here's a welcome activity that will involve the entire class and fill free moments while waiting for lunch, after a lesson or at the end of the day.

Pick a letter—any letter—or ask a student to pick a letter. Avoid the limiting letters such as q, x, z, etc. Then ask all students to write their responses to the following using a word beginning with the chosen letter. Give students 10-15 seconds to respond before moving on.

Invite students to share their responses. Students who have the same answer should cross it out. Discuss the variety of answers. Find out if any students come up with responses that no one has listed. Write their names on the chalkboard for special recognition.

Assure the students that correct spelling is not critical to this activity.

Using the chosen letter, name one:

- city
- country
- girl's name
- boy's name
- fruit
- vegetable
- dessert
- article of clothing
- occupation
- animal
- pet
- flower
- famous landmark
- game or sport
- place to go
- color
- toy
- hobby
- bird
- state or province

Stage Struck

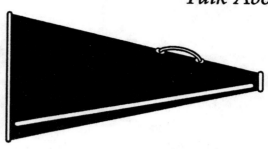

Quick, creative dramatic activities develop self-confidence and encourage children to build verbal skills. Here are some suggestions to try with young actors and actresses.

Vocalize the Part

Practice conveying different meanings and emotions through your voice. Choose a single word for example, and try to express fear, happiness, questioning, serenity, excitement, etc. by changing the way the voice sounds.

Locate a book of short plays or skits with limited characters. Don't worry about props or costuming. Take turns reading the parts and exploring ways to change the way the characters express themselves.

Create simple puppets and invite students to introduce them to classmates.

Select a few poems and ask for volunteers to read the poems aloud.

Choose a song everyone knows. Speak it together instead of singing.

Play the Part

Choose a product and perform a new commercial for television.

Play the role of a game show host. Introduce your contestants. Announce the prizes.

Play the part of an actor or actress receiving an Academy Award. Give your acceptance speech.

Pretend you are a stand-up comic. Tell the class a joke.

You are a radio disc jockey. Introduce the next song to be played.

You are a variety show host. Introduce the next act.

Be a sportscaster. Describe an exciting play "as it happens".

What About You?

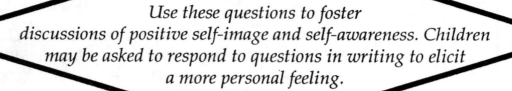

*Use these questions to foster
discussions of positive self-image and self-awareness. Children
may be asked to respond to questions in writing to elicit
a more personal feeling.*

◆ What makes you feel most proud about yourself?

◆ What makes you feel most proud about your family?

◆ What can you do very well?

◆ What do you think is your best strength or feature?

◆ What makes you a good friend?

◆ What would you like to accomplish in your lifetime to help make this a better world?

◆ What do you feel your friends think is most special about you?

◆ What is your special place in your family?

◆ What is **one word** you would use to describe yourself?

◆ If a book were being written about you, what would make a good title?

◆ How do you like to celebrate when you are feeling especially good about yourself?

◆ If you could change one part of yourself, what would you choose to change?

◆ What is the story about how you were named?

◆ What change would you like to see happen in our world in the next ten years?

◆ What gives you great pleasure or enjoyment?

When Is it Better?

*This question boils down to some basic decision-making.
Ask students the questions below. Talk about their responses
and the reason behind their choices.*

When Is it Better to ... ?

... speak instead of being silent

... push instead of pull

... laugh instead of cry

... walk instead of run

... wear tennis shoes instead of sandals

... sign your name instead of print

... use pencil instead of pen

... drink water instead of milk

... eat a small meal instead of a big one

... use a raw egg instead of a boiled one

... use crayon instead of pencil

... rest instead of play

... be patient instead of rushed

... telephone instead of write

... write instead of visit

... ask instead of answer

... think before you speak

... stop before you start

... dream instead of do

... ask for help instead of trying to do it yourself

... be with an old friend instead of a new

... ask a friend for advice instead of an adult

... be perfectly honest instead of holding back the truth

Good Old Days

It's time to talk to an older generation!

Technology has brought many advances that are commonplace in today's world. Computers, video cameras and digital watches are ordinary items in many homes today. Airplanes and automobiles are hardly noticed.

Do your students know about the items found in homes and lives of past generations?

Give them a list of the things below. Get them talking to parents, grandparents and older friends and relatives to find out what these things are and how they were used in the past.

Then get back together to share stories, add to the list, create photo essays or do some more research on inventions and antiques.

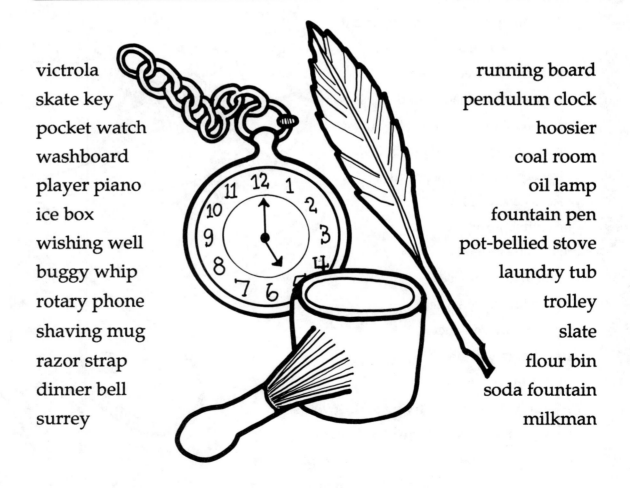

victrola

skate key

pocket watch

washboard

player piano

ice box

wishing well

buggy whip

rotary phone

shaving mug

razor strap

dinner bell

surrey

running board

pendulum clock

hoosier

coal room

oil lamp

fountain pen

pot-bellied stove

laundry tub

trolley

slate

flour bin

soda fountain

milkman

Show & Tell

Kids are never too young or too old to participate in the classroom tradition of show-and-tell.
Just vary the topic depending on the age of your students.
Try some of these.

- Favorite stuffed animal
- New product they've tried
- Advertisement that appealed to them
- Souvenir from a sporting event or play
- Program from a sporting event or play
- Family heirloom (with permission!)
- Hobby or collection
- Handcrafted item
- Special book
- Map of another country, state or province
- Family photos
- Travel brochure from a recent or
    upcoming trip
- Newspaper article
- Information about people or places in other
    parts of the world
- Unique stamp of a letter
- Catalog with unusual products
- Construction blueprints
- Art supplies and techniques
- Newly-learned move in soccer, basketball or
    other sport
- Unusual natural object–a multi-colored rock, a
    bird's nest, an oddly-shaped leaf or shell.
- Meaningful gift from a friend or relative
- Information about community events

•Encourage classmates to ask questions about what is being shared. They
    will become better listeners.

•Encourage children to share frequently. They will build self-esteem and
    gain confidence.

• Promote a variety of sharing topics. Their world will be expanded.

Find Another Way

An important thinking skill to develop is the ability to gather your knowledge and come up with a variety of ways to solve a single problem.

These ways may be out of the ordinary—even imaginative—but they should get the job done.

Here are some unusual situations that need unusual solutions. Try working in groups for some collective brainstorming.

* How could you prepare a meal if the stove is broken?

* How could you travel across country without the use of airplane, train or automobile?

* Where could you get help if your parents aren't home?

* How can you provide lighting if the electricity is out?

* Where can you get research information for a report if you have no materials at home?

* How could you bandage a cut if there are no bandages available?

* What could you fix for dessert that doesn't require baking?

* How could you get in touch with a friend if you have no telephone?

* Where could you go for fun if there was no money in the budget?

* Where would you cross a busy street if there were no traffic signals or crosswalks?

* How could a sport be played fairly if there were no referees or umpires?

* How could you keep food cold if the refrigerator wasn't working?

* How could you carry extra books if you had no backpack?

DECISION DISCUSSIONS

Discuss these instances—some silly, some familiar—in which decisions must be made. Discuss the steps involved in the decision-making process and the compromises that must sometimes be made.. List options together. Learn how to "weigh the options" and come to a final decision

EDIBLE DECISIONS

- Waffles or pancakes?
- Eat out tonight or cook at home?
- Lots of small meals or three big ones?
- Boysenberry or maple syrup?
- Salt and pepper or no seasoning?
- Cake or fruit for dessert?

FRIENDLY DECISIONS

- Ride your bike or skate to a friend's house?
- Ask an old friend or invite a new one to your birthday party?
- Be honest with a friend or protect them from a painful truth?
- One special friend or lots of friends?
- Play with a group of two or a group of three?
- Join a team or participate in an individual sport?

LEISURELY DECISIONS

- Play outside or inside?
- Read a book or watch television?
- See a scary movie or a comedy?
- Check a book out of the library or purchase a copy?
- Repair a broken toy or replace it?
- Take a nap or exercise?

Strictly Classified

Engage in classifying activities that encourage students to apply some creative skills to the skill.

Just Junk

Start a junk box and fill it with buttons, pasta, bottle caps, paper, writing tools, etc.

Examine, sort and group objects. Consider shape, color, texture, uses and other unusual classifying criteria such as with or without holes, material, manufacturing process, etc.

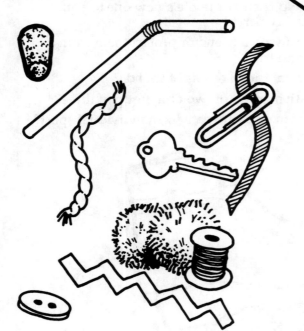

About Animals

Purchase a discounted animal dictionary or encyclopedia. Cut it apart and laminate the pictures. Classify. Consider number of legs, prey or predator, skin color, method of movement, etc.

Consider the Classifieds

Cut apart the classified section of the newspaper. Clip the headings, too. Classify by matching an advertisement to a heading. Consider ads that might fit more than one category.

Grocery Get-togethers

Assemble a variety of empty food containers including cans, jars, and boxes. Keep all labels intact. Consider classification by food groups, packaging, color, meals at which this food is

They might be silly; They might be serious. You might even know that they'll work. Whatever the solution, create some cures for these common—and not so common—ailments, conditions and circumstances.

CREATIVE CURES

BOTHERSOME BODY STUFF

hiccups
toothache
sore throat
common cold
hoarse voice
earache
headache
bad breath
limp hair

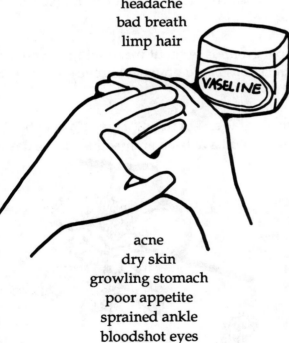

acne
dry skin
growling stomach
poor appetite
sprained ankle
bloodshot eyes
wrinkles
sunburn
chattering teeth
goosebumps
sneezing

NOISY NUISANCES

squeaky wheel
chirping bird
barking dog
crying baby
snoring sleeper
quacking duck
crowing rooster
fighting cats

ANNOYING ACTIONS

losing your house key
absentmindedness
sleeplessness
hunger
boredom
fatigue

Observe This!

> *Students should develop skill in the process of observing as well as gain knowledge of what they observe. Besides these 'starters', provide opportunities for listening, touching, tasting, and smelling observations.*

◆ What color are the principal's eyes?

◆ Sit in a way that your students cannot see your shoes. Suddenly pop the question, "What color shoes am I wearing today?"

◆ Show selected art masterpieces to your students. Have them study the painting for several minutes. Remove it and ask questions on detail. (Focus the questions on obvious elements in the picture.)

◆ Ask students to describe the clothing of the student seated directly behind them. No turning around permitted!

◆ Take a walk with your students around the school grounds without mentioning the purpose. Upon returning to the classroom, ask a host of questions based on what you've seen to test how keenly students noticed what you saw and heard.

◆ Read Helen Keller's essay to your class (suitable for grades 4-6) titled "Three Days to See." In it, she describes what she would like to see if she would have been granted just 'three days to see.' Discuss.

◆ Bring in a fresh flower from the garden or florist. Display it on your desk for the better part of a day. Remove it. Ask your students to write a descriptive paragraph on the flower where the leaves, blossom, color, etc. are detailed.

◆ Ask students "Describe what I wore yesterday."

◆ Set up a "mystery smell" table.

◆ Bring to class a variety of textures—sandpaper, velvet, vinyl—for students to compare and describe.

SOLUTION SLEUTHS

Where do you go, where do you look, who do you ask ...?
... To find answers and solutions to the questions below?

Make a chart of student responses. Categorize by reference materials, human resources or other creative solutions. Encourage them to think of several possibilities for each question.

➡ How would you find out how much a loaf of bread costs in another country?

➡ How would you find the day's high and low temperature in London, England?

➡ How could someone find out the fastest way to drive from their city or town to Montreal, Canada.

➡ What are two different ways to find out how many students there are in your school?

➡ What are three different things to do with games or clothing your family no longer use?

➡ How could you find out where to get a musical instrument repaired?

➡ How could you go about trying to return an expensive piece of jewelry you found to the rightful owner?

➡ How could you find out the city in which you were born?

➡ How would you find out what holidays are celebrated in Japan?

➡ Where could you get more information about upcoming events in your community?

➡ How could you make reservations to travel to another country?

CREATE

Create a new type of sandwich.
Create a new kind of cake.
Create a new name for mustard.
Create a name for the hottest movie now showing.
Create and name the 8th day of the week.
Create and name a new color.
Create a board game for children your age.
Create an all-purpose gift wrap.
Create an unusual dessert.
Create a way to pick up a cactus.
Create a silly song title.

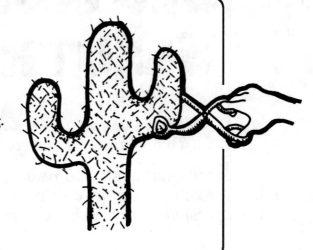

DEVELOP

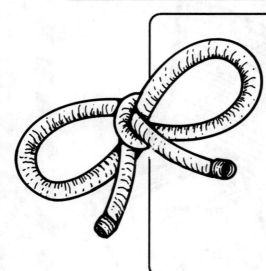

Develop a new way to fasten clothing.
Develop a new concept for a television comedy show.
Develop a lunch or dinner menu using foods that start with the letters d or h or b.
Develop and name a new dance
Develop a new species of flower. Describe and name it.
Develop a dinner menu serving only orange or red or green foods.
Develop 3 new uses for a garden hose.
Develop rules for a new outdoor game.
Develop a way to make house cleaning easier.
Develop a healthy new kind of beverage.

DESIGN

Design a new toy with four wheels.
Design a musical instrument using rubber bands.
Design an invention that would help kids your age.
Design and name a new article of clothing.
Design your dream bedroom.
Design a new automobile.
Design a toy a baby would love.
Design a way to wash an elephant.
Design a foolproof way to keep bread from getting stale.
Design a way to keep a dog warm.
Design a playground that has "something for everyone".
Design a new way to travel.
Design a home for a giraffe.

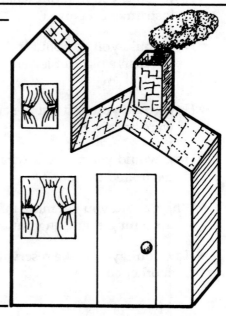

How Would It Be Different?

Pose this hypothetical question to students. Add one of the endings below. Some are silly, some are serious. Discuss, write, form committees and come up with some well-thought-out responses.
Students will need to draw on their abilities to assume, evaluate and hypothesize.

HOW WOULD IT BE DIFFERENT IF ...

... we went to school at night?

... there were no school at all?

... there was no such thing as breakfast cereal?

... there were no stoves?

... there were only adults in the world?

... every country had a king?

... we had no pencils?

... it never stopped raining?

... we had no automobiles?

... insects were as large as people?

... there were no books?

... our only form of transportation was horses?

... children were the parents?

... our parents never said "NO"?

... there were no music?

... we had three arms?

... we were never hungry?

... we didn't have to eat vegetables?

... we all looked the same?

... we all acted the same?

... there were no colors?

... we didn't have holidays?

... there were no colors except white

... there was no gravity?

... there were no clocks?

... we could only eat pizza?

... the wheel was never invented?

... people could fly?

... we never slept?

... there were no telephones?

... the ocean was made of jelly?

... we couldn't cry?

... we used cookies instead of money?

... we had no policemen?

... smiling was against the law?

... there were no stars?

... trees grew candy?

... there were no wars?

... no one had manners?

... all people were selfish?

... snails could run?

... every wish came true?

... we never recycled anything?

... the world was flat?

... there were no teachers?

... water didn't freeze?

... our shadows were alive?

What's the Difference?

In our daily lives, some words are used interchangably even though there are definite differences between them. Draw some conclusions about the differences between the pairs below.

a rug and a carpet

a uniform and a costume

a fence and a gate

a job and a career

a meadow and a pasture

a dish and a plate

an apartment and a home

a boat and a ship

soup and broth

curtains and drapes

a spoon and a ladle

a baby and an infant

an elf and a troll

a jail and a prison

a canyon and a valley

a mountain and a hill

a blackboard and a chalkboard

an illustration and a drawing

a pail and a bucket

a spider and an insect

a butterfly and a moth

snow and hail

a hoe and a rake

a toupee and a wig

a teapot and a coffeepot

Clever Comparisons

Encourage creative thinking by asking your students to contrast and compare the following sets or pairs. How is each item similar and different in appearance, use, habits, function, etc.

➤ a guitar and a violin

- ➤ salt and pepper
- ➤ a puppet and a marionette
- ➤ a portrait and a sketch
- ➤ the forest and the woods
- ➤ freedom and democracy
- ➤ an autograph and a signature
- ➤ a fruit and a vegetable
- ➤ a horse and a zebra
- ➤ ice cream and sherbet
- ➤ sleeping and snoozing
- ➤ a cupboard and a pantry

➤ cupcakes and muffins

- ➤ a warning and a reminder
- ➤ a laugh and a chuckle
- ➤ a dolphin and a porpoise
- ➤ an ocean and the sea
- ➤ solitude and loneliness
- ➤ a compliment and an insult

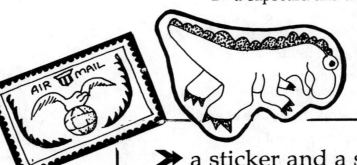

➤ a sticker and a stamp

Before and After

Develop observation, recall and application skills by observing simple changes. Encourage students to describe the look and feel of objects before and after change takes place. Observations can be shared in the form of group discussion or descriptive writing.

Start with some of these …

Dissolve a sugar cube in water.

Make jello.

Add food coloring to water; then stir.

Blow up a balloon.

Beat egg whites until stiff.

Melt an ice cube.

Make frozen lemonade or other juice.

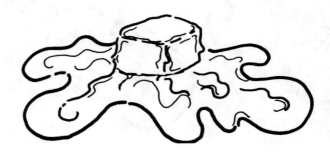

Pop popcorn.

Boil water.

Wind up and play a music box.

Use ribbon to curl or make a bow.

Sharpen a pencil

Blow bubbles with liquid soap.

Blow air through a straw into a glass of water.

Sew a seam in two pieces of fabric.

Punch holes in paper.

Light a lightbulb.

Strike—and put out—a match
    (teacher demonstration only).

Melt a crayon or piece of wax.

Crumple a piece of paper

Chew a stick of gum.

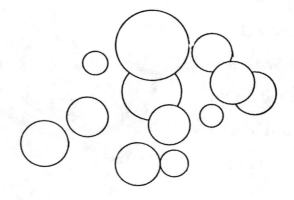

ELABORATE ELABORATIONS

The mind is a wonderful place for picturing detail. Start with these simple statements. Ask students to elaborate, either in writing or verbal discussion, providing as much colorful detail as possible. Share the elaborations as examples of descriptive speech.

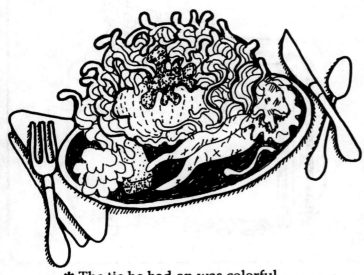

✳ His costume was scary.

✳ That dinner was delicious.

✳ The football game was exciting.

✳ I had way too much to eat.

✳ It was an eventful train trip.

✳ Her new hair style made me chuckle.

✳ The kitchen was really a mess.

✳ The inside of the restaurant was unique.

✳ The tie he had on was colorful.

✳ I couldn't believe what my dog dragged home.

✳ The party decorations were really festive.

✳ The ice cream sundae was an unusual combination of flavors.

✳ The gift was wrapped in the prettiest paper!

✳ The bouquet of flowers was lovely.

✳ Her silly hat was the center of attention.

✳ The closet was extremely organized.

✳ The teddy bear certainly looked well-loved!

✳ It's my idea of a perfect afternoon.

✳ The dinner he fixed was so yucky!

✳ It was my favorite combination of ingredients on that pizza!

How good are your students' memories? Strengthen their abilities and improve thinking skills.

TOTAL RECALL

Make recall and memory a game by spontaneously asking questions that students must respond to immediately—or within 10 or 20 seconds...

• What did you wear yesterday?

• What did I wear yesterday?

• What did you have for dinner last night?

• What grade did you get on your last math test?

• What was on the school lunch menu on Monday?

• Who was at your last birthday party?

• Where did your family go on your last vacation?

The following activities will also present opportunities to strengthen recall skills...

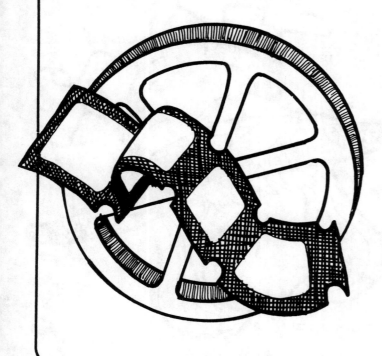

• Read a story to the class. View a filmstrip, film or video. Ask questions based on visual details.

• Arrange for students to listen to a speech. Ask key questions to see if students were listening. Or hand out a list of questions and have them write their answers.

• Work with students who have difficulty in recall...assign short parts in a skit for them to memorize in addition to their cues.

• Assign a favorite class television show for the class to view at night at home. View it also. The next day, ask questions to see how much students recall.

• At the end of a school day, ask children to tell the order of what they did in school today.

Come up with a new . . .
Come up with a new . . .

*Put innovative minds to work. Choose a project;
then share the results.*

➤ *license plate design for your state or province*
  • create the design
  • write a new motto

➤ *kind of sandwich*
  • list the ingredients
  • give it a name

➤ *month*
  • create a calendar page for it
  • give it a name

➤ *color for a box of crayons*
  • name it
  • mix paint to show the color

➤ *planet*
  • locate it in the solar system
  • make a model of it

➤ *writing utensil*
  • describe its use
  • make a list of its benefits

➤ *name for a car design*
  • Illustrate a magazine ad for it
  • describe its special features

➤ *breakfast cereal*
  • design a package for it
  • create an advertisement

Creative Investigations

Animal Investigations

Delve into the interesting world of animals. Spark interest with the questions and followup activities below. The extent of their research will depend on their level.

- What kind of tracks do animals make?

- What species are currently endangered? What is being done to save them?

- What is animal camouflage? Draw pictures of animal camouflage.

- Locate a copy of the *Guiness Book of Animal Records*. Learn an astounding new fact every day.

- What sounds do animals make? Make a list of the words used to describe animal sounds.

- How are animals classified? Learn to pronounce a few of the classifications.

- What kinds of homes do animals build? Make a model, mural or poster depicting an animal's home.

- How does the food chain work in the animal kingdom? List ways the food chain helps make the world a better place.

- What do animals see? Pretend you are a particular animal and describe the world through your eyes.

- What are the biggest and the smallest animals in the world? Make a chart that shows at least ten animals, ranked in size from largest to smallest.

- Choose an animal category—mammal, insect, bird—and make a mural of at least ten animals that fit the category.

- How do people hunt animals? Debate the issue of hunting.

- What animals are found in Africa? Write a journal from the point of view of a traveler on a safari.

- What animals are found in other regions—mountains, tropical forests, grasslands? Create lists and compare inhabitants for similarities and differences.

- What animals live in the deserts? Write a travelog from the point of view of a caravan traveler.

- What are some of the chores that animals perform? Play a pantomime guessing game.

- How do animals use their bodies to protect themselves? Illustrate some of these body features— horns, quills, claws, etc.

OUT OF THIS WORLD!

Use these activity ideas and space/astronomy questions to motivate students for independent study on the planets, our solar system, astrology and space exploration.

What are the names of the planets?

What is the Big Dipper?

What does UFO stand for?

Where is the Johnson Space Center? the Kennedy Space Center?

Would you rather visit the moon or Mars? Why?

Who was the first woman to go into space?

What is astrology? What are the 12 astrological signs?

Make a graph of students' astrological signs. Study personality types for each sign. Have students decide if they are accurate for everyone.

Have a class debate: "Astrology is absurd vs. Astrology is scientific."

Visit a planetarium.

Design and name a new robot.

Have a **Science Fiction Festival**...read a book, design a poster.

Create an original Star Trek script and dramatize it.

Visit an air and space museum.

Get a class subscription to "Odyssey"-Space Exploration and Astronomy for Young People- Kalmbach Publishing Co., Waukesha, WI.

Create a current events bulletin board of recent news articles dealing with space travel.

Write to **NASA** for any free available classroom materials.

Map Pursuits

Maps can open a whole new world of learning.
Here are some map activities and a host of related projects.

✤ Make maps that illustrate historical events:

  ✤ Trace the trail of Lewis and Clark.

  ✤ Chart the seas for the voyage of Christopher Columbus (or any other ocean-going explorer).

  ✤ Map the route of the first transcontinental railroad in your country.

  ✤ Retrace Paul Revere's famous ride.

  ✤ Locate all the battlegrounds of World War II, the Civil War or any other war.

✤ Create Global Awareness. Give each of several groups of students, a map of a country in the news. Ask them to hunt through newspapers and magazines for current articles related to that country. Keep a notebook or create an area on a bulletin board for each map and the collected information. Allow time for current event discussion.

✤ Explore the variety of maps available...topography, road, resource, population, etc. As a class project, choose a country, state or province. Divide into committees. Assign each committee a different kind of map to create for the chosen country. Assemble all maps into a notebook.

✤ Utilize reference materials that name the deserts, volcanoes and mountains of the world. Locate them on a map.

✤ Study a product resource map from a country. Set up a table that displays some of the resources from that state, country or province.

✤ Calculate the distance between cities.

✤ Learn to read a map's legend. Create some innovative legends and corresponding maps. (Candyland, Sports Country, etc.)

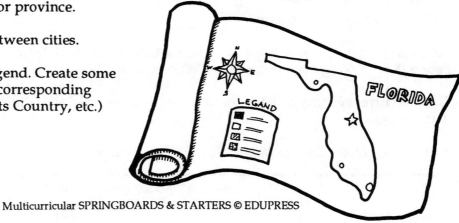

FLAGS AND FACTS

Send students on a flag fact-finding assignment. Display a large poster of international flags. Have encyclopedias and other reference materials available for students to use.

Discover:

Which countries have flags with only vertical stripes?

How many countries have flag with only two colors? three colors?

Which countries use only red, white and blue in their flag?

Which country has a flag of one solid color, with no stars, stripes, symbol or insignia?

Which countries have a flag with one or more stars, but no stripes?

Which countries have a flag that uses a combination of stars and stripes?

Which countries have a flag with a symbol or emblem?

What country's flag uses the most colors?

What color is used most often?

How many have stars?

Do:

Select a country's flag to research. Report on the meaning of the flag's features.

Choose flags to color and duplicate. String all the flags on a yarn line across the classroom.

Research the flag of the state or province in which you live. Find out the history of the flag's design. Draw a picture of it. Is there a motto? If yes, what is it?

> Here's a way to provide students with the opportunity to pursue multicurricular learning independently.
>
> Invite them to select an area of interest and then, following some structured guidelines, find out more.

Encourage Independence

Follow these steps:

1. Provide a list of themes, topics, interests and subjects from which to choose. Give students an opportunity to contribute ideas and brainstorm a list together.

2. Give each participating student a copy of the contract on the following page. Explain the guidelines. Suggest some activities in each curriculum area.

3. Allow students some time to think about their topic. Encourage them to discuss it with family members. Ask them to choose a theme they are really excited about.

4. Ask students to complete their individual contract by checking a choice in each category and writing a one-sentence description of what their project in each curriculum area will be.

5. Conference with each student to review their theme and projects. Be sure the projects they have selected are appropriate to their individual learning level. You may want to limit the number of projects a student needs to complete to satisfy the contract.

6. Discuss how progress reports will be handled. Suggest ways they might share their exciting learning with classmates.

Here's a list of very broad theme areas to get you going.
Add specific subjects in each category.

- Musical instrument
- Cars
- Prehistoric times
- Clothing
- Dolls
- Sports
- Hobbies

- Cooking
- Other countries
- Arts and crafts
- Travel
- Animals
- Outer space
- Monsters

Independent Project

Name:

Theme/Topic:

Conference:

~~~~~~

Check one activity to do in each assigned category.
Write a short sentence that tells about it.

1. ## Reading

❑ fiction   ❑ non-fiction
❑ magazine   ❑ book display
❑ poem   ❑ other

_____

_____

2. ## Writing

❑ poem   ❑ story
❑ letter   ❑ book report
❑ news report   ❑ other

_____

_____

3. ## Research

❑ fact list   ❑ interview
❑ oral report   ❑ vocabulary list
❑ timeline   ❑ other

_____

_____

4. ## Social Studies

❑ map   ❑ photo essay
❑ news article   ❑ oral report
❑ scrapbook   ❑ other

_____

_____

5. ## Math/Science

❑ experiment   ❑ display
❑ chart   ❑ demonstration
❑ word problems   ❑ other

_____

_____

6. ## Art

❑ painting   ❑ drawing
❑ mural   ❑ diorama
❑ craft   ❑ other

_____

_____

~~~~~~

Encourage Independence

Provide students with the opportunity to develop and demonstrate problem-solving skills initiative, independence, and original thinking.

These ideas will achieve that goal plus give students a chance to contribute to the classroom and classmates.

❈ Design a current events bulletin board; Then keep it up to date.

❈ Organize and manage a "Lost and Found" department for classmates' belongings.

❈ Develop an activity to add to a learning center. Demonstrate its use.

❈ Create a "Welcome to our Classroom" packet for new students. Include schedules, school map, "homework help" phone numbers, and names to contact for after-school activities.

❈ Decorate a recycling bin for leftover art project materials; Then develop an activity based on the contents collected in the bin over a period of several weeks.

❈ Write a worksheet for the class to complete.

❈ Design a bulletin board. Plan the materials and carry it through to completion.

❈ Submit a story title or starter for creative writing.

❈ Develop a list of topics to research .

❈ Create a welcome sign for the classroom door.

❈ Develop a system—including instructions—for turning in work.

❈ Organize a "class improvement" committee to listen to and enact on constructive suggestions.

❈ Prepare an art project for the class to participate in. Make a list of materials; Gather the materials; Demonstrate the procedures.

❈ Donate some time to organize book shelves, storage cabinets and coat closets.

❈ Teach a new outdoor or indoor game.

❈ Develop a vocabulary/spelling list derived from a literature selection.

❈ Select a book to read to the class.

❈ Create a display of books related to a subject being studied in class.

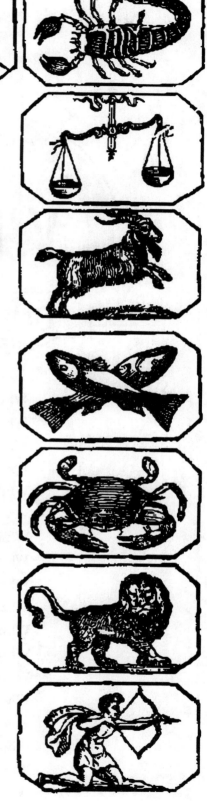

Exploring Sun Signs

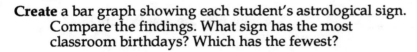

Familiarize students with the 12 signs of the zodiac. Use the following activities to find out if the moods and minds of your students are 'in sync' with these signs.

Create a bar graph showing each student's astrological sign. Compare the findings. What sign has the most classroom birthdays? Which has the fewest?

Find out which category each sun sign belongs to:
• Air • Water • Earth • Fire
How many students' astrological signs are in each category?

Make a list of the generalized personality traits for each sign. How do students feel they "fit the mold" of their sign? Is there another sign they fit more closely? Theorize why this might be so.

Cut out horoscopes from newspapers and magazines. Evaluate whether your horoscope for the day was on target or not. Practice writing your own horoscopes.

Have each student paint their astrological symbol. Decorate a bulletin board, create a mural or build a wall border with the finished paintings.

Relate the astrological signs to the calendar. How do the months of the year fit into the astrological chart?

Research the history of astrology.

Discuss the merits of astrology. Is it something that can be believed and followed? Why? Why not?

Find out which signs your best friends fall under. Do you see any pattern in your selection of friends or those with whom you get along the best?

Challenge your students to be detectives and find out the people who are the "WHO" in each question below.

Offer a question as an opener in the morning. At the end of the day, ask the detectives for their solution. Find out what clues they followed to get to the answer.

Who was in love with Juliet?

Who discovered Australia?

Who made the first airplane flight?

Who was the first Private Eye?

Who painted the *Mona Lisa?*

Who was the first to fly over the Atlantic Ocean?

Who invented the telephone?

Who headed the famous "Round Table".

Who assisted Dr. Watson?

Who loved Maid Marian?

Who kissed the girls and made them cry?

Who is Diana Spencer?

Who became the first woman to serve on the
　　　Supreme Court of the United States?

Who invented the automobile?

Who had a little lamb?

Who created Disneyland?

Who lives in Buckingham Palace?

Who lives in The White House?

Who was the first American to walk on the moon?

Who wrote *Macbeth?*

Who was the most famous Antarctic explorer?

Who hunted for the Seven Cities of Gold?

Initials Are Everywhere

You see them on television, you see them in advertisements, you see them on signs.

What do these familiar initials stand for? Look in books. Ask friends. Ask parents. Ask anyone you see. Write your findings in the space next to each.

TWA

AT & T	PBS
GM	N.Y.C.
UPS	D.C
ABC	JFK
CBS	ERA
NBC	PTA
CNN	FBI
MCI	CIA
BMW	UN
TWA	FDR
USPS	LBJ
KFC	GI
BBC	UK

SIMPLY KNOWLEDGE

Sometimes it's fun to just "know stuff".
Here are some intriguing questions that should get intriguing answers.

Ask a question on Monday. Allow the rest of the week for students to research the answer.
Spend some time on Friday discussing the answers.
Encourage students to bring photos, articles and other information to add to the lively discussion.

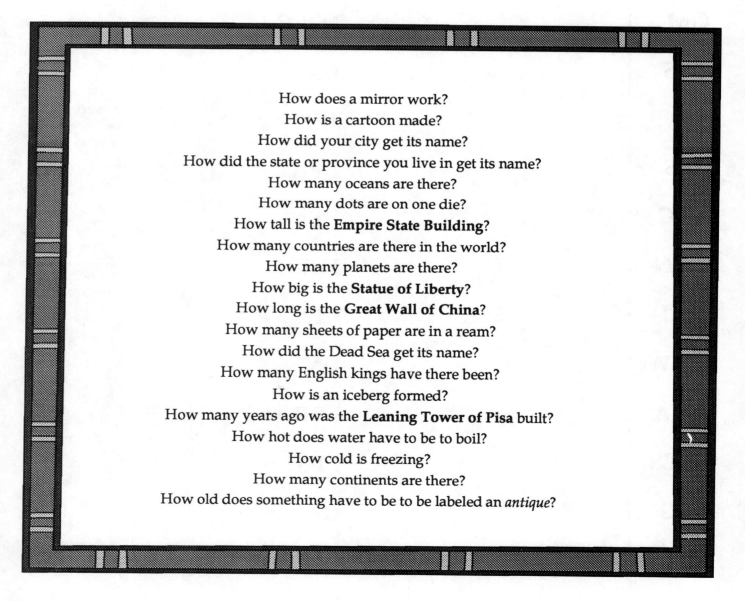

How does a mirror work?

How is a cartoon made?

How did your city get its name?

How did the state or province you live in get its name?

How many oceans are there?

How many dots are on one die?

How tall is the **Empire State Building**?

How many countries are there in the world?

How many planets are there?

How big is the **Statue of Liberty**?

How long is the **Great Wall of China**?

How many sheets of paper are in a ream?

How did the Dead Sea get its name?

How many English kings have there been?

How is an iceberg formed?

How many years ago was the **Leaning Tower of Pisa** built?

How hot does water have to be to boil?

How cold is freezing?

How many continents are there?

How old does something have to be to be labeled an *antique*?

What Is? ... What Are?

*Quick questions to find answers to will provide research
opportunities for students of any age or ability.
Find out what these things are ... Share your findings.*

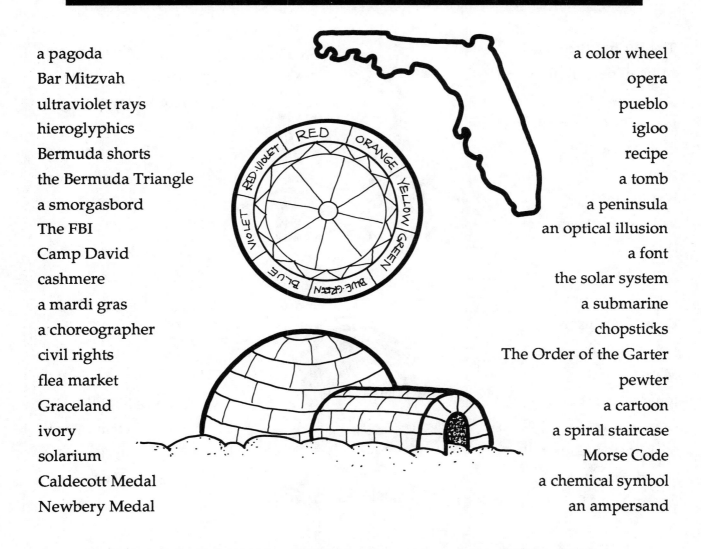

a pagoda

Bar Mitzvah

ultraviolet rays

hieroglyphics

Bermuda shorts

the Bermuda Triangle

a smorgasbord

The FBI

Camp David

cashmere

a mardi gras

a choreographer

civil rights

flea market

Graceland

ivory

solarium

Caldecott Medal

Newbery Medal

a color wheel

opera

pueblo

igloo

recipe

a tomb

a peninsula

an optical illusion

a font

the solar system

a submarine

chopsticks

The Order of the Garter

pewter

a cartoon

a spiral staircase

Morse Code

a chemical symbol

an ampersand

Who Is? ... Who Are?

*Quick questions to find answers to will provide research
opportunities for students of any age or ability.
Find out who these people are ... Share your findings.*

The Wright Brothers

Mikhail Baryshnikov

John Newbery

Hans Christan Andersen

Howdy Doody

Prince Rainier

Napoleon

William Shakespeare

Aesop

Amelia Earhart

Carl Sandburg

Emily Dickinson

Louis Braille

Marc Chagall

Johann Strauss

Clara Barton

Sir Winston Churchill

Socrates

Barnum and Bailey

Michelangelo

Abbot and Costello

Frank Lloyd Wright

Montezuma

Neil Armstrong

Sally Ride

Beethoven

Louisa May Alcott

Alexander the Great

Anne Boleyn

Gainsborough

Galileo

Julius Caesar

Nehru Gandhi

Florence Nightingale

Henry Ford

Albert Einstein

Samuel Clemens

Nero

Where Is? ... Where Are?

*Quick questions to find answers to will provide research
opportunities for students of any age or ability.
Find out where these places are ... Share your findings.*

The Statue of Liberty

The Eiffel Tower

Lake Pontchartrain

The Catskill Montains

Muir Woods

Sahara Desert

Potomac River

Northwest Territory

Longwood Gardens

Leaning Tower of Pisa

Taj Mahal

Niagara Falls

The Green Mountains

San Andreas Fault

Easter Island

The Parthenon

Big Ben

Windsor Castle

The Hague

Appalachian Trail

White Cliffs of Dover

Notre Dame

Great Pyramid

Mount Fuji

Pentagon

Palace of Versailles

Kremlin

Great Wall

Yukon Territory

Yosemite

Old Faithful

Haleakala Crater

Hoover Dam

Nile River

Grand Canyon

Alps

The White House

The Great Barrier Reef

Quick Questions

Start with a "quick question". Discuss the various resources students can use to help them find the answer. Expand student knowledge by challenging them to complete one or all of the learning extenders below each question.

What is a foal?
1. Make a list of "baby" animal names.
2. Make up a game that matches baby animal names with the adult animal name.
3. Draw a picture of a foal.
4. Find out about the care and feeding of a foal.
5. Find pictures of different kinds of horses.

What is a celebrity?
1. Make a list of celebrities.
2. Choose a celebrity and write a biography.
3. Which celebrity you would most like to be?
4. List the different kinds of celebrities (sports, movies, politics, etc.). Find one in each category.
5. Keep a scrapbook filled with articles about and pictures of a celebrity of your choice.

What is the difference between an alligator and a crocodile?
1. Make a list of other reptiles.
2. Draw a picture of an alligator or a crocodile.
3. Find out in what parts of the world alligators and crocodiles can be found.
4. List four facts about each of these two reptiles.
5. Make a picture chart of several reptiles.

What are the names of the Canadian provinces?
1. Draw a map of Canada. Label the provinces.
2. Choose one province to research and create a display or write a report.
3. Gather travel information about one province.
4. Make a list of the capital of each province.
5. Find two books at the library about a province and share it with classmates.

What country uses a drachma as a unit of money?
1. Define the word *currency*.
2. Create your own system of currency.
3. Find out about one other country and the type of currency it uses.
4. Bring a sample of money from another country to share in class.

What is *mah jongg*?
1. Learn to play a new card game.
2. Find out about a card or board game from another country.
3. Make your own mah jongg game. Learn to play.

Quick Questions

Here are more "quick questions" and learning extenders for students to research, explore and talk about. Encourage students to make oral presentations that share their discoveries with classmates and spark cooperative learning.

What is an earthquake?
1. Define *epicenter*.
2. What is a *seismograph* and how does it work?
3. How are earthquakes measured?
4. Draw what the lines on a seismograph would look like if registering an earthquake magnitude of 7.2.
5. Draw a map that shows the path of the *San Andreas Fault*.

What is a rain forest?
1. Make a chart showing some of the animals that can be found in a rain forest.
2. Find out how people who live in a rain forest survive.
3. Paint a mural or large picture of what a rain forest looks like.
4. Describe three of the plants or trees that are found in a rain forest.

What is the difference between the Arctic and the Antarctic?
1. What is a *tundra*? What is it found?
2. Make a chart of penguins that can be found in the Antarctic.
3. Locate the Arctic and Antarctic on a globe.
4. Define *iceberg*. Draw a picture of one— above and below the surface of the water.

What is animal camouflage?
1. Make a list of animals that are able to camouflage themselves.
2. Find pictures of animal camouflage. Share them with classmates.
3. Research different kinds of camouflage. Write a sentence or short paragraph describing each.
4. Find out how insects camouflage themselves.

How is an *aquarium* different from a *terrarium*?
1. Fold a piece of paper in half. On one half, show pictures of what is found in an aquarium. On the other half, draw what is found in a terrarium.
2. Make your own terrarium.
3. What plants are best for an aquarium?

What is a *hajji*?
1. Locate the city of Mecca on a map.
2. Find out three facts about Moslems.
3. Why do Moslems face in a certain direction when they pray?
4. What is the *Kaaba*?

Clothing Connections

Throughout history, people have worn different types of clothing. Students can learn a lot about another country,culture by researching the clothing worn.

Spark their interest with these clothing connections.

RESEARCH

- purpose
  religious, ceremonial, decoration
- protection
- customs
- available material
- historical era

PROJECTS

- puppet
- draw a picture
- create the costume and wear it
- photo essay
- dress a doll
- collage of magazine pictures

PROFESSIONS

Choose a profession. Find out about clothing needed for

- safety purposes
- uniforms
- appropriate wear

CATEGORIES

- hats and headgear
- shoes
- traditional clothing
- national costumes

DESCRIBE

- *turban*
- *chadri*
- *kimono*
- *serape*
- *sarong*
- *sari*
- *toga*
- *poncho*
- *veil*
- *sabots*
- *kilt*
- *chaps*
- *manta*
- *obi*
- *panung*

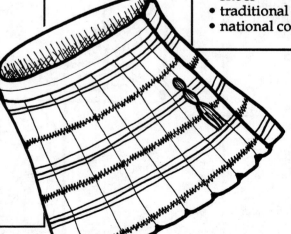

What's It Made Of?

We all handle, use and eat dozens of different things every day. Did you ever wonder what they were made of? Well, it's time to find out. Do some research and exploration to find out what these items are made of. Write your discoveries in the space under each one. Share your findings with classmates.

birdseed

ice cream

glass

lipstick

hairbrush bristles

ink

glue

cellophane wrap

sauerkraut

soap

gum

cola soda

candle

raisins

potpourri

battery

golf ball

pencil

Read-Aloud Roundup

The benefits of reading aloud to children are many. Not only is the wonderful world of books opened to curious minds but good listening skills are encouraged, too. Don't leave a stone unturned in your search for exciting and interesting read-aloud material. Consider books and periodicals in many categories. Some are suggested below.

Book Categories

Adventure
Humor
Sequels
Series
Anthologies
Aesop's fables
Fairy Tales
Stories from other lands
Nature poems by Robert Frost
Growing up stories
riddles and jokes
Folk tales
Mythology
Courageous acts and people
Biographies
Autobiographies
Science fiction
Career information
Specific authors
Records and amazing feats
Non-fiction
Space travel
Geography
Hardy Boys
Nancy Drew
Legends
Poetry
Chapter books
Mystery
Literature Classics

Variety

Newspaper articles
Magazine articles
Sports trading cards
Art prints
Plays
Recipes
Travel brochures
Encyclopedias
Comic Strips
Almanac
Greeting cards
Advice columns
Photo captions
Pictorial essays

> *It's thrilling to see what you've written ...*
> *... **in print!***
> *Provide lots of opportunities for children to share their writing success. Here are some suggestions for turning classroom writers into published authors!*

Let's Get Published

- ✏ Publish a classroom newspaper. Write stories, create headlines, add cartoons and edit classified ads. Distribute to other classes and send copies home to parents.

- ✏ Write letters to local newspapers, commenting on events in the community.

- ✏ Place an ad in the classified or personal sections. Talk to your local newspaper publisher to see if you can print for free. Explain your author's program!

- ✏ Write press releases of classroom activities to send to newspapers or local newsletters.

- ✏ Establish a school-wide **AUTHOR'S CORNER.** Decorate a bulletin board in a highly traveled part of school such as the office or cafeteria/auditorium. Invite other classes to post their authors' efforts.

- ✏ Create class novels. Work together to write and edit. Then reproduce, bind, and display on a bookshelf for classroom visitors to enjoy.

- ✏ Place completed writing in an author's basket. Gather the class together frequently to share the basket's contents. Invite students to read their writing aloud.

- ✏ Publish a schoolwide literary magazine. Ask your parent/teacher organization for help and financing.

- ✏ Write resumes and post them on a job-market bulletin board.

A Starter...
... At the Start

> Here are some sparks to get creative writing started. Give students an opening sentence. Brainstorm some possible plots. Encourage them to be imaginative. Students complete the story and create a title for it.

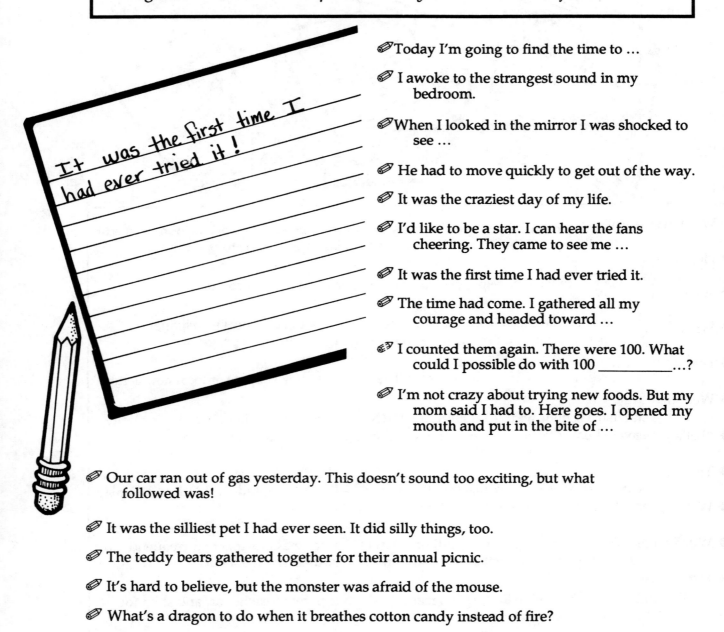

It was the first time I had ever tried it!

✐ Today I'm going to find the time to ...

✐ I awoke to the strangest sound in my bedroom.

✐ When I looked in the mirror I was shocked to see ...

✐ He had to move quickly to get out of the way.

✐ It was the craziest day of my life.

✐ I'd like to be a star. I can hear the fans cheering. They came to see me ...

✐ It was the first time I had ever tried it.

✐ The time had come. I gathered all my courage and headed toward ...

✐ I counted them again. There were 100. What could I possible do with 100 _____...?

✐ I'm not crazy about trying new foods. But my mom said I had to. Here goes. I opened my mouth and put in the bite of ...

✐ Our car ran out of gas yesterday. This doesn't sound too exciting, but what followed was!

✐ It was the silliest pet I had ever seen. It did silly things, too.

✐ The teddy bears gathered together for their annual picnic.

✐ It's hard to believe, but the monster was afraid of the mouse.

✐ What's a dragon to do when it breathes cotton candy instead of fire?

✐ "They don't know I can talk," thought the puppy. "I'll wait until just the right moment to say something."

A Starter...
...At the End

> *"Story Starters" have become a favorite tool in creative writing. Try this new twist with the same idea—only now your students are given the ending or final sentence and they must create everything that comes before it to make the given ending meaningful.*

➜ From then on the two girls spoke to each other on the phone three times a day.

➜ Who would have ever believed that the morning started off so badly!

➜ I was so glad I listened to Mom and didn't resist. What a surprise!

➜ It's funny how wonderful things happen when you least expect them!

➜ I'm sure Dad is saying once again, "I told you so."

➜ It was worth getting into trouble. I never had more fun!

➜ Will I ever learn???

➜ He had always been my very favorite until that day.

➜ What would you have done?

➜ What a weird way to spend a birthday!

➜ I can't believe how easily I got fooled.

➜ Well, that's the real me!

➜ "Let's get together sometime!"

➜ Then she said, "STOP!"

➜ Walking three miles in the rain does wear you out.

➜ Will I ever stop laughing?

➜ It's a funny world all right.

➜ Then everyone started singing.

➜ So I said "good night" and went up to bed.

➜ It was a vacation we'll remember for a long time. I sure am glad to be home.

A Different Point of View

Use words, pictures or roleplaying to adopt a different point of view. Discuss the expression "Standing in someone else's shoes..." Talk about how that might change the way you looked and felt about something.

*Then offer these ideas for students to practice viewing the world from another's perspective. Remember to encourage them to consider both visual **and** emotional outlook.*

OCEAN
through the eyes of...

- a fish
- a sailor
- a fisherman
- a surfer
- a whale
- an artist

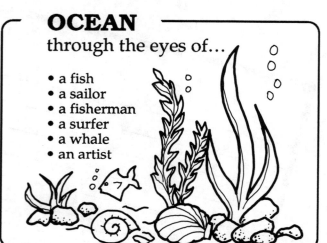

SKY
through the eyes of...

- an astronaut
- a sky diver
- a planet
- a bird
- a pilot
- a cloud

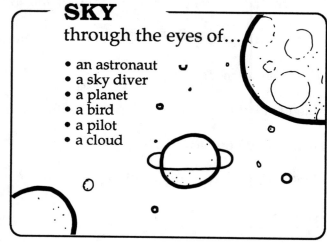

RAIN
through the eyes of...

- a farmer
- a bird
- a camper
- an umbrella
- a plant
- a homeless person

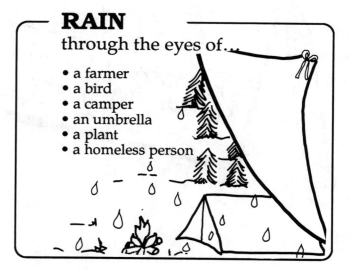

DESERT
through the eyes of...

- a scientist
- a camel
- a pioneer
- a lizard
- a cactus
- a hiker

An Imaginative Point of View

Now use words or pictures to imagine what you can't see. Practice visualizing possibilites—both practical and imaginative.

Extend the possibilities to different levels of thinking. Apply facts, information, intuition and creativity!

What's on the

OTHER SIDE OF

- a wall
- a mountain
- a lake
- a fence
- a bridge
- a tunnel

What's at the

BOTTOM OF

- the ocean
- a pit
- a volcano
- a hole
- a mine shaft
- a bucket

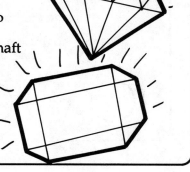

What's at the

END

- a train track
- a country lane
- the subway line
- a rainbow
- a treasure hunt
- a dangling string

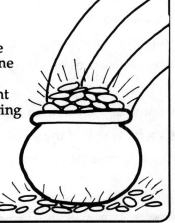

What's

INSIDE

- the earth
- a prehistoric cave
- a squirrel's tunnel
- a pharoah's tomb
- a hiker's backpack
- a rocketship

Tell About Television

Here's an activity—one time or weekly—that turns students' television time into productive learning time.

Choose a program within one of the categories below. Send students home armed with a copy of the report form on the following page. They may select any program during the week but they must watch and report carefully.

... morning news program   ... documentary

... evening news program   ... cartoon

... daytime talk show   ... sporting event

... movie suitable for age group ... travel show

... situation comedy   ... current event show

Use the reports as springboards for a host of other television-related activities:

- Create a new cartoon character.
- Present a newscast to be video taped in class.
- Make a list of programs appropriate for viewing.
- Make a list of the negative—or positive—influences of television.
- Brainstorm six topics for a talk show program.
- Plan six questions a show moderator could ask about each topic .
- Form small discussion groups with students who watched the same program.
- Share current events heard during televised newscasts.

Tell About Television

Report Form

STUDENT NAME: _____

CATEGORY: _____

PROGRAM VIEWED: _____

DATE AND TIME: _____ CHANNEL: _____

Who were the leading characters? Give their show names. Describe the personality of one of the characters. If this was a news program other program with a host, hostess or anchor person, list their real names. Describe their physical appearance.

_____

_____

_____

Write a summary of the show. Ask yourself "What was the main idea?" "What did I learn? " If the program was a comedy, tell about two of the events. If you watched a news, cooking, travel or sports show, what was the main feature?

_____

_____

_____

_____

_____

What is your opinion of the show?

_____

_____

_____

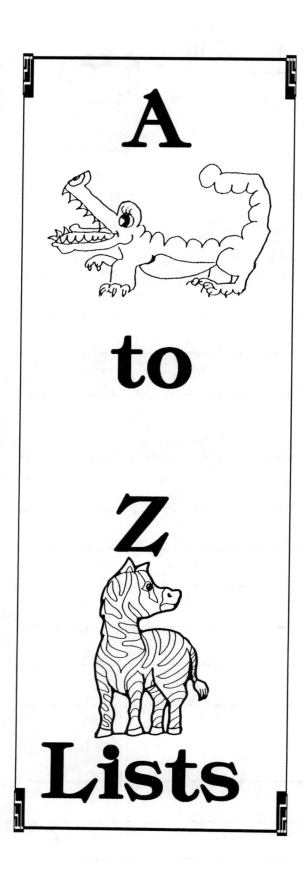

Here's a different approach to research and responses! Assign a category; then ask students to create a list from **A to Z**.

Work in teams or alone. Award "prizes" from **A to Z**—apple, book, cupcake etc.—for complete and imaginative lists.

Once students "get the hang of it", making lists will be an easy assignment starter!

A to Z List Categories

◆ action verbs
◆ adjectives
◆ animals
◆ boys' names
◆ cities
◆ clothing
◆ colors
◆ countries
◆ desserts
◆ events
◆ famous people (last name)
◆ flowers
◆ furniture
◆ food
◆ girls' names
◆ hobbies
◆ holidays
◆ ice cream flavors
◆ inventors (last name)
◆ kitchen tools
◆ occupations
◆ places to go
◆ song titles
◆ sports
◆ toys
◆ verbs

Quick Picks for PARAGRAPHS

As student writing skills improve, keep them busy writing paragraphs. First be sure they understand the elements of a good paragraph. Use these prompts below as paragraph writing subjects.

Paragraphs can also be illustrated and displayed in an easy-to-make bulletin board.

Write about ...

... One of the five senses

... today's weather

... how a turtle protects itself

... things that quench your thirst

... the benefits of watching television

... the parts of a tree

... the best kink of pet

... a delicious sandwich

... places to go in your city

... a club or team you belong to

... things to do when you're sick

... favorite things about school

... a visit to the doctor or dentist

... something you did over the weekend

... your neighborhood

... your house

... an event to remember

... why you like skateboarding, skiing, bicycling, etc.

... what you know about dinosaurs

... a hamburger's ingredients

The best sandwich I have ever tasted....

Things to do with paragraphs ...
- read aloud and identify the topic sentence
- copy on the chalkboard and proofread together
- make comparisons

DAFFY DEFINITIONS

Create definitions for these deliciously daffy words. Assemble the responses into a classroom **Daffy Dictionary**. Start with the word list below. Ask students to create their own words to expand the dictionary.

Try exchanging definitions and challenging other students to use the newly defined word in a sentence.

Ask older students to expand on their definitions by dividing the word into syllables and assigning a part of speech to it.

muzzlewafer	conkervision	deroder
wrinkleslop	jetster	opperhum
storf	lineomatic	plastermast
kinkler	freelie	crunkle
scareascope	charsicle	wimpledot
frickalink	mupple	kalitch
gurky	coltch	dudbum
gigglehunk	stringdoo	cluzzelduff
wurspit	quirkyblast	grencoal
skyszx	draxcess	beandrop
singabopper	ratchist	cresky
slome	bicklebee	chocoplast
slamp	slooper	zeer
popalopper	dwaddle	phunder
eeping	wifflewaffle	frizzlehump
thrump	diffy	wackyrod
lugpump	vegetater	scutchy
tappity	guish	waferwoof

POETRY PROJECT

Write a page for each of these poetic forms. Bind the pages together with a decorated cardboard cover. Strengthen the spine with book binding tape.

COUPLET

A *couplet* is two lines of poetry that rhyme. Each line should have about the same number of syllables.

Couplets can be joined together to make a longer poem.

> *My dog Jed*
> *Goes to Club Med*

FREE VERSE

Free verse has no set form. Usually there is no rhyme pattern. The poet is allowed to be very creative.

> *I small chocolate and cookies baking in the oven. I see new things and happy people eating cookies and having fun. I feel the love in the air .*

CINQUAIN

A *cinquain* is a five-line poem.
- Line 1 has one word. It is the same as the title.
- Line 2 has two words and describes the title.
- Line 3 has three words and describes action.
- Line 4 has four words that describe feeling.
- Line 5 has one word and refers to the title.

> *Snail*
> *Slimy, slippery*
> *Moving, climbing, sleeping.*
> *Weird looking thing.*
> *Hermaphrodits.*

HAIKU

A *Haiku* is a poetry form with its origin in Japan. It describes something in nature.

> *Wind blows in my face.*
> *Quietness in the airness*
> *In the afternoon.*

The samples accompanying each form were written by a third grade student, Leanne Milliken.

Ask students to write a mini-book about someone—past or present —who has impressed them by their accomplishments.

The Assignment

The booklet should include a page for each of the following:
- biographical information
- descriptive paragraph summarizing the person's accomplishments
- a photograph, sketch or photo copy of the individual
- related pictures, magazine or news article
- fact list
- cover

The Candidates

president
prime minister
world leader
military leader
explorer
inventor
astronaut
musician
sports personality
monarch
famous child
movie star
television star
politician
dancer

The Follow-up

- **Present** the booklets in a short oral report.
- **Read** a variety of biographies.
- **Brainstorm** an expanded list of "people" nouns.
- **Compare** the difference between nouns and proper nouns.
- **Create** a cooperative PERSONAL HERO mural.
- **Share** the booklets in a cross-age program.

LOTS of Literature Ideas

Sometimes you need just a quick followup activity to tie into a literature selection. Here are some ideas. Suggested grade level is indicated in parentheses.

🐾 ***Zoophabets;*** Robert Talon. Scholastic (2-3)

Summary: *Inventive creatures, from Alpok to Zurk, detailing where they live and what they eat.*

Followup Activity: Compile your own dictionary of imaginative, alliterative animals. Ask each class member to contribute a page.

🐾 ***Animals Should Definitely Not Wear Clothing;*** Judi Barrett. Atheneum (2-3)

Summary: *Imgine animals in clothing! You'll see and read about them in this book.*

Followup Activity: Illustrate pictures of animals in creative ensembles.

🐾 **C.L.O.U.D.S.;** Pat Cummings. Lothrop (3-4)

Summary: *A designer of the skies earns some appreciation from a young girl.*

Followup Activity: Use watercolor paints to create a "designer" sky.

🐾 ***How the Camel Got His Hump;*** Rudyard Kipling. Bedrick(3-4)

Summary: *Back when the world was new, a lazy camel is set straight by the magical Djinn of All Deserts.*

Followup Activity: Create folk tales for other animals. "How the Elephant got his trunk." "How the Kangaroo got her pouch ."

🐾 ***How Big Is a Foot?*** Rolf Myller. Atheneum (3-4)

Summary: *The lack of a standard measurement results in an unusual bed for a king.*

Followup Activity: Find a variety of ways to measure things in the classroom. Share the problem-solving techniques that were devised.

🐾 *A Chocolate Moose for Dinner;* and/or

🐾 *The King Who Rained;* **Fred Gwynne.** Simon & Schuster (4-5)

Summary: *Older students will appreciate speech taken literally, as narrated by a young boy who misunderstands them. .*

Followup Activity: Illustrate your own play on words. This will require some dictionary digging by the students.

Pique student interest in a book by starting with a prop. Choose a prop related to the book selected to read aloud and put it on a table set aside for just that purpose—introducing a new literature selection. Share the prop and brainstorm possible plots, characters and story twists. Read the story together.

Table Top Story Prop

How close was the actual story to your plot "predictions"?

Students will look forward to that empty table being "filled".

Here are some suggestions. Appropriate grade level ad related activity are indicated.

BOOK:
Chester the Worldly Pig by Bill Peet (gr. 2-3)
A fame-seeking pig runs away to join the circus and winds up on all seven continents.

PROP/Activity
world globe/Locate the seven continents.

BOOK:
The Lemonade Trick by Scott Corbett (gr. 3-5)
Kirby and his chemistry set change good boys into bad, and vice versa.

PROP/Activity
lemonade mix, pitcher, cups/Mix up some lemonade and share a glass.

BOOK:
The Toothpaste Millionaire by Jean Merrill (gr. 4-6)
Rufus challenges the business community by marketing a product called "toothpaste".

PROP/Activity
tube of toothpaste/Talk about oral hygiene.

BOOK:
Twenty-One Balloons by William Pene duBois (gr. 4-6)
Adventures of a professor who sails around the world in a balloon.

PROP/Activity
21 balloons/Give 21 children a balloon to blow up.

BOOK:
How to Eat Fried Worms by Thomas Rockwell (gr. 3-4)
A bet to eat a worm a day for 15 days with a $50 payoff is accepted by Billy, who claims he can eat anything.

PROP/Activity
gummy worms/Munch on a gummy worm
OR a real worm in a jar/Examine the worm through a magnifying glass.

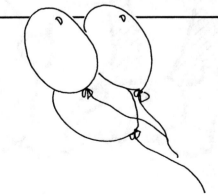

Table Top Story Prop

BOOK:
The Good-luck Pencil by Diane Stanley (gr. 2-3)
"Whoppers" written for a school assignment backfire when a pencil renders them real.

PROP/Activity
pencil stubs/Write tall tales.

BOOK:
The Treasure Trap by Virginia Masterman-Smith (gr. 4-6)
Two feisty kids dig up their yard in search of a millionaire's missing cash that disappeared.

PROP/Activity
small shovel, dirt in a box, play money/Create a treasure map complete with instructions and directionals.

BOOK:
Two Bad Ants by Chris Van Allsburg (gr.3-4)
View the world through the perspective of two adventursome ants.

PROP/Activity
ants in a jar or an ant farm/Observe the activitiy of the ants.

BOOK:
Alistair's Time Machine by Marilyn Sadler (gr. 3-5)
Built for the science fair competition, a time machine takes Alistair to past eras.

PROP/Activity
clock, nuts, bolts, batteries/Take an imaginary trip in a time machine. Where would you go?

BOOK:
Everybody Needs a Rock by Byrd Baylor (gr. 2-3)
Ten rules for finding the perfect rock..

PROP/Activity
assortment of rocks/Ask each student to indicate his or her favorite and tell why.

BOOK:
The Mice Who Lived in a Shoe by Rodney Peppe (gr. 1-3)
A many-member mouse family constructs a safe new home using a human shoe as the frame.

PROP/Activity
several different shoes/Look for pictures that show shoes worn around the world (wooden, snow, sandals, etc.)

BOOK:
The Chocolate Touch by Patrick Skene Catling (gr. 2-3)
A boy's passion for candy leads to a magical affliction. Everything that touches his lips turns to chocolate.

PROP/Activity
chocolate candy/Imagine a plot twist and write about it. (Everything turns to rubber or gold or green)

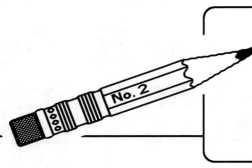

Writing Projects

Here are some ideas for projects that will provide students with "more-than-a-story" writing opportunities:

Greeting Cards

Make it a tradition to write over-sized greeting cards to fellow classmates who are celebrating birthdays or are ill. Write a "get-well" message along with your signature.

Autograph Books

Staple several pages together to form a booklet. Allow students time to sign their name and write short messages in each other's autograph books.

Editorials

Write a letter to your local newspaper expressing your opinion about something in the community.

Words to Live By

Rewrite your favorite sayings, proverbs or words of wisdom in a journal. Use them as springboards for discussion and motivation.

It's a Fact

Start *fact scrolls*. Hang several lengths of butcher paper on the wall. Write a different heading in large letters at the top of each scroll. Number the scroll vertically. Invite students to research and write a fact under the heading.

Some heading ideas include:
• individual flowers, plants or animals.
• people and places
• specific sports or athletes
• countries, cities or landmarks

Fairy Tale Twists

Even students who have passed the age of reading fairy tales may enjoy these challenging activities where they can put their imaginations and creative thinking skills to use.

Create a display of favorite and popular fairy tales. Encourage students to spend some time acquainting themselves with these classic stories.

- Pretend the seven dwarfs are ladies—not men. Rename them !

- Change the image and name of *Goldilocks and the Three Bears*. Create a character in place of Goldilocks who is either a redhead or a brunette. Give her a suitable name. Create three other animals for Goldilocks to encounter. How would the story change?

- The wicked witch in *Snow White and the Seven Dwarfs* is tired of her "Mirror, mirror one the wall, Who's the fairest of them all?" rhyme. Write a new one for her.

- *Jack and the Beanstalk* tells about a country boy who traded his cow for some magic beans. What if Jack were a city boy? What might he trade? What might he get for the trade? Create a story twist based on these new circumstances.

- Imagine that the color red is not in fashion this year. *Little Red Riding Hood* needs her wardrobe brought up to date. Design a new outfit for her. Create a new name for this fairy tale based on the new design.

- The girls may pretend they are *Cinderella;* the boys are Prince Charming. Search through clothing catalogs and magazines for the outfits they would wear to the ball. Cut them out and paste them in a simple display.

Getting Along in Groups

Working cooperatively in small groups may have its share of problems. How do you deal with sparring students? Friends who fight? Group members who don't get along?

Start with these ideas that are intended to show students they can work out their differences.

Start with Something Pleasant

• Pair up for a pleasant task where students need to rely on one another. When its time to work, they should feel confident that, even though they aren't good friends, they can depend on each other to get a job done.

Find Something Good

• Ask each student in the group to list three things they like about each group member.
"He has a nice smile.
" His handwrtiing is very neat.
" He is kind to his friends.
• Exchange lists and let group members read the positive things others have to say. When they learn that others are aware of their good qualities, students will be more apt to be confident in a group.

Discover Common Interests

• Spend some time talking about yourselves before group work begins. Students may find they share common interests and communication will become easier.

Let's Be Open

Openly discuss the problems that two students in a group might have. Encourage other group members to freely stop the squabbling members and tell them their actions are annoying.

You're In Charge

Appoint a group chairman who has the right to report differences and disputes that can't be resolved to the teacer. Make the chairman the final decision maker.

NETWORKING NOTIONS

"Live and Learn."
"Learn from the mistakes of others."
"Experience is the best teacher."

These sayings were created for a reason! Find out why in your classroom. Network with others to share and learn. Here are some ways to get started.

Network with your local offices of government and community services.

- Attend a city council meeting.
- Invite the mayor to visit the class to discuss projects goals and dreams for the community. Invite students to share ideas.
- Trade jobs for a day. Select a student or small group of students to be mayor, building inspector or law enforcement officer for the day. Travel with these officials as they attend to their duties. Report the experience to classmates.

Network with other classes

- Cross-age tutor
- Share a reading hour
- Create a list of "book favorites" to copy and share.
- Become pen pals with a class from another school. Exchange ideas for successful classroom activities and theme experiences.

Network with your school's parent organization

- Set up a suggestion box. Meet and discuss the ideas with organization leaders.
- Find out ways to help with school fund raising projects and learn about business at the same time.

Network with local businesses.

- Enlist your local yellow pages. Invite business owners to visit your classroom to share the "tools of their trade." Learn how to make a floral arrangement. Practice a new dance step. Find about health foods that are available. Invite an exercise specialist to share the lstest in fitness techniques.
- Ask for donated items—discontinued books, art supplies, etc.—in return for student-created advertising flyers and posters.

Network with each other.

- Set up a homework helpline.
- Establish a telephone hotline. Pass along last-minute information.
- Implement buddy-system. Help each other with assignment dates and other classroom responsibilities—be a friend.

Committee Concentrations

This form of cooperative learning activity requires that ALL students in the group contribute to the assignment.
Here are some prompts to get committee inquiries going.

THINK of a new idea for a television situation comedy. Propose a title, setting and list of characters.

DESIGN an effective poster for bicycle safety.

ORGANIZE a new service-oriented group. Present the goal and decide on its first service project.

CREATE an effective slogan to emphasize water conservation. Design bumper stickers, buttons and other promotional items.

PLAN a new route for an explorer in today's times. Chart his or her course and list the necessary supplies.

CREATE a day's worth of balanced menus. Present them in a picture mural.

OPEN a restaurant. Plan the menu, design the decor, decide on a name.

CHOOSE an invention to research. Make a time line of its history. Research the ways it has changed our lives.

INVESTIGATE the world of insects. Choose one to research, diagram and present in a photo essay.

EXPLORE the five senses. Create an activity for each. Share them with the class.

FIND OUT ABOUT a religion. Make a short presentation. Talk about the traditions and beliefs.

COMPILE interesting current events. Create a bulletin board or poster that displays the articles. Be prepared to summarize them to the class.

CREATE a mural using materials, theme and methods decided on by the group.

CHOOSE a type of tree to research. Make a photo essay showing how it looks, the shape of its leaves, foods derived from it and uses for its material.

SELECT a book and present it as a newscast. Interview main characters. Report on the WHO•WHAT•WHERE•WHY•WHEN.

PLAN three projects based on shadows. For example, present a pantomime, create shadow artwork, measure shadows at different times of the day.

WRITE and present a short skit about personal hygiene.

PRESENT a fashion show. Write the descriptions, decide on models and moderators. Plan a clothing theme. For example, *Silly Play Clothes; Cool Outfits; Super Funky Sweatshirts.*

PRACTICE and present a choral reading to the class.

MAKE a time line of events over a period of 100 years.

CREATE a giant tissue paper mosaic. Work together to sketch, cut and glue. Decorate the room with the results.

DEVELOP a list and display of favorite books to report on and share with classmates.

RETELL a fairy tale, complete with outfits and shortened plot.

WRITE a book about the subject of your choice. Each group member should contribute a page.

Committee Concentrations

Paired Performances

Try these new and innovative methods as students learn to work with a partner—either by their choice or having a partner assigned or picked at random. (To pick a partner at random place each student's name on a small folded piece of paper; place in paper bag and have each student dip in and select a slip indicating partner's name for a particular project.)

• • Have partner pairs select a poem of their choice. Allow time in class (or they may work cooperatively after school) to practice the poem orally, alternating the lines. Poem need not be memorized; reading it is permitted but they should practice speaking their lines for an effective presentation.

• • Have partner pairs select a pair of characters from a book of their choice—dress like them and then read a sleection from the book where each character reads and speaks his/her part.

• • Allow partner pairs to put on a skit or comic presentation. Free choice of partners and of material is the key to an open-ended surprise presentation for this activity.

• • Assign partners (one strong/one less strong student) to teach the class a 'how-to' activity. Partners work out the presentation between themselves.

Paired Performances

•• Assign partner pairs to work together on a report. This may be a good hidden opportunity to pair a strong student with a weaker one to 'tutor' research and writing skills. Partner pair should receive one grade for both students.

•• When planning your next class party, assign students in pairs to be responsible for different tasks. Create a "Party Partner" chart and list names and tasks.

•• Have partner talent day. Let partner pairs practice and perform a song, a dance, modeling clothing, playing musical instruments or any other entertainment of their choice where both students perform.

•• Have "Partners at Play" time. Students are permitted to bring games suitable for playing in pairs. Allow students to play a game with a partner and then move on to play another game with another partner. (An excellent rainy day activity!)

•• Brainstorm with the class to come up with names of famous pairs in television, film and entertainment. Who was the stronger of the pair? Did one always play the patsy or the weaker one?

•• Allow partner pairs to work on a joint art project. Display results on a bulletin board titled "Partners in Art" or "Art Partners." Each work should be signed by both artists.

COOPERATIVE COMPILATIONS

Engage in some compiling projects that involve all your students. These activities call for students to contribute ideas, resources and donations from home.

PHOTOS ON PARADE

Ask each student to bring in a baby photograph. Have children identify it on the back. Post all photos on a "baby bulletin board". Include a caption question such as "Can you find Sarah?" or "Where is Daniel?" Change the caption frequently.

ENVELOPE INVOLVEMENT

Start a collection box of postage stamps cut from letters families receive during the year. Encourage students to bring in the postmarked envelope. Locate the origins on a map or globe. Duplicate the stamps in an art project and arrange around the room.

WE'RE GAME

Have students ask their parents to describe their favorite childhood game so that they can teach it to the rest of the class. Try learning a different game each week during your physical education class or indoors on a stormy day.

SUBJECT SCRAPBOOKS

Select a subject. It might be a/an

- type of building such as a castle or museum

- person such as a famous leader or athlete

- issue such as gun control or the environment

Gather magazine photos and articles, newspaper clippings, related information.

Assemble the material in a scrapbook.

BABY BOOM

Start a chart that compiles information about the birthplaces of students' parents. Send home a short form asking parents to complete the state or province, city and country where they were born.

Graph the results. How many parents were born in the same state, province or city where they now live? How many were born in another? How many similarities and differences are there?

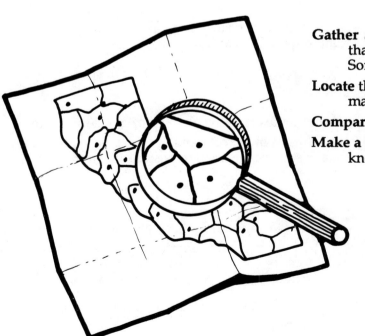

MAP MOGULS

Gather all the road, city and state or province maps that parents or relatives are willing to part with. Sort them by country, state or province.

Locate the regions on a larger world map. Examine the maps for a variety of features.

Compare your findings.

Make a list of cities students have already heard of or know something about.

COOPERATIVE COMPILATIONS

ART All Together

Creating artistic projects together can be a low-stress way to introduce students to cooperative learning projects.

☆ Experiment with a variety of brush widths and paint colors to create a free-form mural.

☆ Tear construction paper scraps into different shapes then glue to poster board

☆ Design a mural based on a novel the class has just read.

☆ Create a bulletin board based on a given topic for a school corridor . Try bicycle safety, junk food, latest clothing trends, anti-drugs, library information, famous artists, underwater life, space exploration or a patriotic display.

☆ Ask each member of the group to contribute "art starters" from home. Some suggestions: varieties of papers; assorted fabric swatches; wallpaper samples, discarded greeting cards, buttons, ribbon. Put the collection into a large bin or bax and ask the group to create some form of art—picture, sculpture—from the contributions.

☆ Provide a large strip of butcher paper on which each student signs his or her name in the most artistic and creative way they can imagine.

☆ Design a creative get-well card for an ill student in the class.

☆ Save and make a creative display of envelopes with humorous or incorrect mailing information,unusual postage stamps, distinctive postmarks, more than eight stamps, etc.

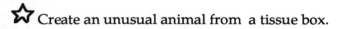

☆ Create an unusual animal from a tissue box.

☆ Design and illustrate some unusual clothing:
- a wild pair of socks
- unique sunglass frames
- a distinctive pair of mittens
- a new hat style

☆ Provide supplies for each group to create its own design of a particular item such as: totem pole, magic tree, flower garden, flag, school banner, patchwork quilt or landscape.

☆ Mix paints to create some "original" colors. Then paint a large mural.

The Sporting Life

*Physical education provides the basis for active group learning.
Here are some springboards for sporty investigations.*

BALL BASICS

• What kind of ball—rubber, basketball, baseball, kickball—can be bounced the most in a minute?

• What kind of ball can bounce the highest? Experiment with different degrees of strength behind each bounce, too.

• What's the farthest a basketball, baseball, kickball, etc. can be thrown?

• What tricks can you teach each other to make catching or kicking a ball easier?

RUNAROUND

• Which is a faster method of movement— run, skip, hop, leap or jump? Test the theory with a variety of combinations from the group.

• Practice running bases together. Give each other tips on how to improve the time.

• Have running relay races. Plan the strategy together. Who should run first? last? Root for each other.

ROPE ROUNDUP

• What is the average number of jumps, before missing, made by the group?

• What's the most number of times someone can jump the rope in a minute?

• Make up a new jump rope chant. Teach the rest of the class.

• Practice single, double and triple jumping. Be supportive.

MORE THAN A MONKEY

• Time a trip across the monkey bars.

• Help each other do "just one more" pull-up.

• Help each other balance on the bar.

SPORTY CREATIVITY

• Design an obstacle course.

• Teach a partner a new skill.

• Create rules and a name for a new game. Teach the rest of the class.

Play a game of "Animal, Vegetable or Mineral". Divide into groups and try to be the first to categorize the given item correctly. Score one point for a correct answer. Subtract one point for an incorrect answer. Have reference books available. Encourage students to research their answer.

Start with the list below; then challenge students to add to it.

Animal, Vegetable or Mineral?

cork	cotton curtains	cherries
wool hat	seweed	cactus
marshmallow	man's beard	chocolate
penny	chewing gum	nylon
paper clip	rubber band	hair
glass	milk	newspaper
envelope	leather shoes	water
gold earrings	orange juice	sand
automobile tire	balloon	crayons
plastic drinking straw	wooden toothpick	coffee
silk scarf	bacon	pearls
peach pit	marbles	candles
ostrich feather	aluminum foil	egg
magazine	fur coat	pencil lead
grass	key	candy cane
lettuce	velvet	duck

Scavenger Hunt

Scavenger hunts can be fun and learning-filled!

Give each class member a bag and a copy of the list below. Divide them into groups. Set a deadline of three to four days for gathering the items. All hunting must be done on student's own time, away from the classroom.

Allow time each day for the groups to meet and share what they've collected. They'll need to discuss, measure, analyze and apply knowledge to determine which item is best for each category. They'll also need to update their lists and decide on the best plan for collecting the still-needed items.

Find something

- ❏ round
- ❏ that makes noise
- ❏ you take on a picnic
- ❏ square
- ❏ made of plastic
- ❏ made of rubber
- ❏ with a pointed end
- ❏ used for measuring
- ❏ used for stirring
- ❏ that operates with batteries
- ❏ used in construction
- ❏ made of wood
- ❏ with holes in it
- ❏ longer than 4 inches (10 cm)

- ❏ found on a birthday cake
- ❏ a bird would like
- ❏ that feels rough
- ❏ that grows on a tree
- ❏ with a diameter less than 2 inches (5 cm)
- ❏ used in sewing
- ❏ that turns
- ❏ found in a desk
- ❏ with a pleasant smell
- ❏ used for decorating
- ❏ that is a bright color
- ❏ for a baby
- ❏ that will hold liquid
- ❏ used to set a table

Notes:

Volunteer Ventures

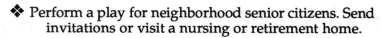

*Build self-confidence and take pride in sharing. Check with local clubs and other organizations for ways to contribute, as a group, to the improvement of your community or to help others who are in need. Make it a one-time or an ongoing project. Every little bit **does** help!*

❖ Perform a play for neighborhood senior citizens. Send invitations or visit a nursing or retirement home.

❖ Honor an Armed Forces veteran.

❖ Share a holiday treat with senior citizens. Sing songs, make cards, bring handmade gifts.

❖ Arrange for groceries to be donated to a needy family.

❖ Volunteer to do housework for an elderly, disabled or infirmed individual; rake leaves, mail letters, walk the dog, etc.

❖ Make and take some edible treat to the local fire station.

❖ Prepare and display posters to promote bicycle safety.

❖ Design a get-well card for an ill student or staff member.

❖ Choose a nearby park—or the school playground— and challenge yourselves to keep it litter-free for the year.

❖ Adopt a grandparent. Share stories and tutoring.

❖ Plan a book and magazine drive. Donate them to a local hospital, library or convalescent home.

❖ Start an year-round food bank to contribute to homeless shelters.

❖ Gather second-hand blankets, shoes and clothing to donate to homeless shelters or needy families.

❖ Recycle in the classroom. Donate the proceeds to a community cleanup project.

❖ Paint the town—decorate store windows for the holidays—free of charge.

FUND RAISING

Sponsor some money-making activities for your class or school.
Spend the proceeds on a needed addition—library books, art supplies, maps, for example—or for something for the community.

Be sure to approve the project with the school administration before implementing any plans.

❖ Collect used books to sell at a "playground" sale.

❖ Collect used dolls and toys to sell to invited guests.

❖ Prepare a benefit puppet or talent show. Charge a small admission.

❖ Wait for warm weather then have a car wash.

❖ Make holiday related crafts to sell at a craft show.

❖ Place art projects on consignment at local gift shops.

❖ Design an insignia for your school. Have it printed on t-shirts or bookcovers to sell.

❖ Conduct an auction. Sell goods and services donated by class members and their parents.

❖ Print a school newsletter. Sell "newsstand" copies.

❖ Sell raffle tickets for a grand prize—perhaps an artistic work or other class-created project.

❖ Grow potted plants and vegetables to sell to non-green-thumb parents and school staff.

❖ Challenge parents or staff to a sporting event—basketball, soccer, kickball, etc. Charge admission to the event.

❖ Compile class recipes. Print and bind together in a booklet.

❖ Have a penny-power day. Ask for donations.

❖ Have a "guess-the-number-of-chocolate-kisses-in-a-jar" contest. Ask participants to pay to enter.

❖ Play bingo. The charge for a game card is a new book for the classroom.

Whole-class INVOLVEMENTS

Sometimes there is power in numbers! Rather than dividing into smaller groups, pursue some activities as a class. Provide students with the opportunity to develop relationships with a variety of students, too. Here are some ideas.

TRAVEL BROCHURE

This travel brochure is about a most unique location—*your classroom*. Assemble this brochure then use it as a guide for parents or other visitors to your classroom. Also revise it for use at Open House. Update the information as it changes. Include:

- Information about the inhabitants
- Points of Interest; things to see
- Map

TREE BUFFET

Research and plan a tree-feast. Each class member should contribute a food grown on trees. Include a variety of nuts, dates, pineapple, apples, oranges, plums etc.

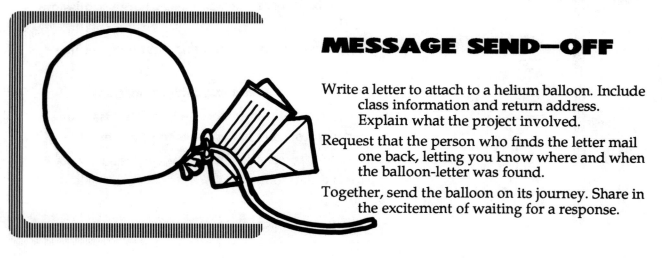

MESSAGE SEND–OFF

Write a letter to attach to a helium balloon. Include class information and return address. Explain what the project involved.

Request that the person who finds the letter mail one back, letting you know where and when the balloon-letter was found.

Together, send the balloon on its journey. Share in the excitement of waiting for a response.

BOWLING TOURNAMENT

Take part in a monthly bowling tournament in which there is only one team—*the class*.

Purchase an inexpensive bowling set from a toy store. Learn the rules of bowling and how to score a game.

Each class member gets a turn. Add the score after each person's turn. Don't forget how to add strikes and spares. Post the class bowling score after everyone has had a turn. Try to beat the previous month's score during the next month's tournament. Enjoy the challenge and practice some math skills—*as a group*.

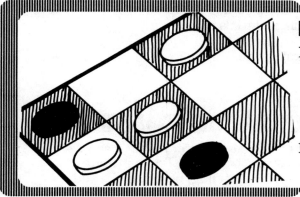

BUILD A GAME CENTER

Recycle board games that families no longer want. Work together to create a center that everyone can use. Teach each other how to play checkers or chess. Get involved in a group game involving buying, selling and banking.

Involve everyone in the care and upkeep of the center.

REMODELING PROJECT

Create a floor plan and move the classroom furniture. Decide together who is sitting where. Discuss the reasons behind the decisions. Find out if a student-created arrangement encourages better classroom cooperation than a teacher-created one.

Decide on a plan for classroom maintenance. Create a list of responsibilities; Then create the crews that will carry out those tasks. Reevaluate frequently.

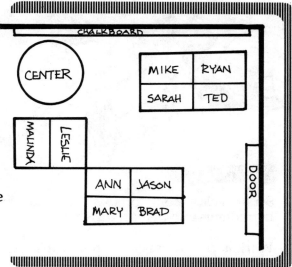

Whole-class INVOLVEMENTS

SCIENCE EXPLORATIONS

> *Set up a mini-lab in a corner of your classroom and encourage your students to spend some free time with scientific explorations. Change the lab's focus periodically and be sure to stock the lab with a variety of books on the subject. Here are some lab suggestions.*

ENVIRONMENT

Bury a small glass jar, a tin can, plastic container, piece of styrofoam and a newspaper page in a large bucket of dirt. Dig them up every couple weeks and compare their decomposition rates. Experiment with other disposable materials.

Design a new, ecology-oriented package for a common product.

Invent a use that will recycle styrofoam containers.

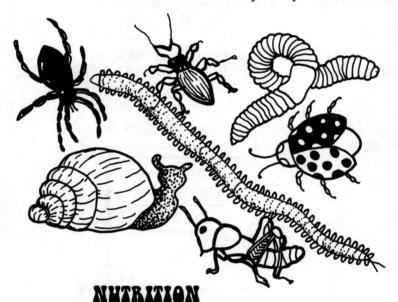

ANIMALS AND INSECTS

Fill the mini-lab with "crawling creatures"— in containers, of course! Try to include a snail, spider, ladybug, worm, snake and grasshopper. (The children will be happy to help with the collecting process.) Compare the way each moves. Do they fly, slither, crawl, hop?

Place a mirror in the bottom of a box. Set several snails on the mirror. (Be sure to put some "greens" in the box for the snails to eat.) Examine the way the snails travel. Time their progress. Draw pictures of snail trails. Use a magnifying glass to look at a snail's slimy trail more closely.

NUTRITION

Set up a classroom "product" lab and learn about vitamins and nutrients. Compare label ingredients and determine which foods have the best nutritional content.

Work in committees to plan several meals. Compare menus. Select the most balanced and nutritious meal to prepare together for a class feast.

S imple S cience S parks

Use these questions as general research activities. Then stimulate students to explore their particular interest further by offering "in-depth" suggestions. Encourage them to experiment and investigate on their own.

What are the parts of a flowering plant? Draw and label them.
- Select several flowers to dissect and examine.
- Make a chart comparing petals, leaves and other plant parts.
- Create a flower coloring book for classmates.

What is a volcano? What causes it to erupt?
- Locate active volcanoes on a globe or map.
- With adult assistance, experiment with baking soda or other substances that might yield an eruption or bubbling effect.
- Make a model of a volcano.
- Find out about disasters involving volcanoes.

What is a constellation? How many are there?
- Find out about the origins of their names.
- Make a chart of the constellations using glow in the dark paint.
- Borrow or find a telescope to view the stars.
- Visit an observatory.

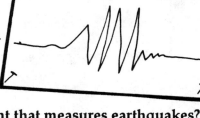

What is the name of the instrument that measures earthquakes? How does it work?
- Recreate a seismology chart during an earthquake.
- Find out about a career as a seismologist.
- Learn about earthquake preparedness.

How does the sun help us? How does the sun hurt us?
- Experiment with different objects in sunlight. What are the effects?
- Conduct a sunblock research project. Which creams are most effective?
- How hot is the sun? Compare its temperature with other objects that have heat.

What are the three major classifications of rocks?
- Make a display of different rocks. Label them.
- Conduct an experiment that shows the effects of different non-toxic liquids on rocks.
- Learn about the job of a geologist.

Social Studies Subjects

Use these topics for brief or in-depth research reports. Students can work independently or in groups to foster cooperative learning. Present reports in written or oral form. Encourage support projects such as pictorial essays, charts or posters depicting an event.

The Eskimo culture

The history of the United Nations

A Native American tribe

Current worldwide event

A woman in history

An invention

Changes in transportation

A past or present world leader

A branch of government

Slavery

An explorer

A form of transportation

Religions of the world

The life of a famous artist

The life of a famous musician

Wonders of the world

Famous landmarks

National Parks

Current event

An era in history

Traditions of another country

A capitol city

Facts about the Pyramids

Life in the city

African tribal life

Popular customs

Clothing from other countries

A European castle

A sport in another country

Folk singing or dancing

A king or queen

A famous battle

Food from another country

A famous statue

Back in Time

Students of all ages will enjoy learning about life in past eras and civilizations.

Talk with the entire class about basic needs: food, clothing, shelter. Divide the class into groups. Ask each group to select a time in history—in their own country or another—and create a project that depicts something from that time period.

Each group then presents their project, along with historical background information, to the rest of the class.

Here are some project suggestions to get students started. They may choose from this list or think of an original idea.

Prehistoric Times
• cave painting murals
• stone mortar and pestle
• rock painting
• bone carving

Ancient Egypt
• model of a pyramid
• hieroglyphic scroll
• headdress
• beaded collar
• loincloth

Ancient Rome
• olive branch wreaths
• model of the colosseum
• togas
• clay sculpture

Medieval Times
• model of a castle
• stained glass window
• jousting exhibition
• life size drawing of a knight

Native Americans
• bow and arrow
• shaman mask
• model of a pueblo or tipi
• picture writing

Frontier Life
• charcoal brands
• western wear
• demonstration of how to pan for gold
• model of a sod home

Geography Gems

Go on a geographic name search to find cities and towns that have special names. Research may be limited to a state, province or country.

Ask students to find names of cities and towns that have the prompts below as the entire name or are contained within the city or town name. For example, Roseville would be acceptable as a town with a girl's name.

Locate a city ...

… with a girl's name

… with a boy's name

… with the name of a flower or plant

… with a President's or Prime Minister's name

… named after an explorer

… named after a king

… that begins with St.—shortened for Saint

… that begins with "Fort" or shortened to "Ft."

… with two words, the first being NEW

… that has a French name

… that has a Spanish name

… with Native American meaning

… named for a Native American tribe

… with more than ten letters

… with less than five letters

… beginning with the word "San"

… that is so common you can find it six times on the map

… with a color word

… with a classmate's name

… with an animal name

LAND or SEA
Dictionary

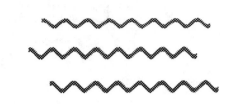

As children learn about the world they read aboutbodies of water, landforms and other geographic features. However, the differences may not be focused on and students may not know what makes each one unique. Here's an activity to resolve the situation. Students may work cooperatively to complete the assignment.

Have your students research the definitions of bodies of water and landforms. Create a dictionary or booklet with each one featured on a page.

The page should include these elements:
- heading—word being defined
- illustration
- definition sentence or short description
- page number

Here's a list of words to choose from. Specify the number of pages each dictionary should have.

LAND

village	desert		
hamlet	volcano		
town	region		
city	crater		
state	butte		
province	cliff		
country	mesa		
island	plains		
peninsula	valley		
continent	cave		
mountain	reef		

SEA

pond	ocean
lake	gulf
brook	waterfall
stream	iceberg
delta	glacier
river	estuary
canal	wave
strait	tide
bay	inlet
harbor	channel
sea	spring

SPELLING WITH 𝕻𝕴𝖅𝖅𝕬𝖅

> *When spelling lessons need a "pick-me-up", try these activities for variety.*

Word 𝕻𝖎𝖟𝖟𝖆𝖟!

✱ Involve students in selecting their spelling words. Ask them to make lists based on an activity, a current literature selection, a sport, current event or other category. When a student's list is used, feature him or her as the "Speller of the Week".

Writing 𝕻𝖎𝖟𝖟𝖆𝖟!

✱ Bring art and spelling together. Create a simple design by drawing squiggly horizontal and vertical lines Write a spelling word in each space. Decorate each space around the words.

✱ Fold a piece of paper into four columns. Try these heading variations. List spelling words in the correct column:

adjective	adverb	noun	verb
1 syllable	2 syllables	3 syllables	4 syllables
3-4 letters	5-6 letters	7-8 letters	9 or more letters

✱ Make up a poem using all your spelling words.

✱ Create a crossword puzzle using your spelling words.

✱ Include as many of your spelling words as possible in one sentence.

✱ Write a nonsense sentence for each spelling word. Take turns reading the sentences aloud and share the laughter.

Spelling with PIZZAZ

Picture Pizzaz!

✱ Find pictures in magazines to illustrate the spelling words. Make little booklets with the pictures pasted above the written word. Place one picture per page. Write a caption that includes the word, to describe the picture.

✱ Print each word. Draw a box around each letter. Now write the words using only the boxes. Identify the word.

✱ Cut out letters from magazines and put them together to spell the words. Paste the letters for each word onto construction paper. Choose colorful letters of different types and sizes. Make this spelling poster bold and beautiful.

✱ Paint a mural of spelling words. Outline the letters; fill them with colorful patterns; design starbursts around each one.

Pair Pizzaz!

✱ Work in pairs. Each student scrambles the spelling words and gives the list to their partner. Starting at the same time, unscramble the words. Who can finish first? Trade papers again to check correct spelling.

✱ Make up a clue for each spelling word. Read the clue to a partner. The partner guesses the word then spells it correctly.

✱ Write a short two-player script that uses all the words. Present the script to the class. Ask them to keep track of how many of the words were used.

Reading POWER

Here are some starters intended to motivate students to read.

Book of the Evening Club

Store books in large envelopes marked with the book title. Tape a check-out list to one side. Invite students to check out an envelope to take home for an evening. Ask them to share a little about the book they read during opening activities the following morning.

Half-Way Reading

Read half a book, just enough to arouse curiosity. Leave the book on the chalkboard ledge or book shelf for students to pick up and finish on their own.

Pair up for reading. One student reads the first half of a book. Another reads the second half. Report on the book to the class, with each student summarizing the half he or she read.

Reading Prescriptions

Keep a note pad handy for writing reading prescriptions to give to your students. For example:

Read 6 pages at bedtime.

Read 4 pages, every three hours.

Read 7 pages each morning.

Beat the Book Report Blues

Let students tell you, for a change, what method they would like to use to report on a book they've read. Suggest displays, posters, videos, photo essays. Ask them to brainstorm other ideas to choose from. Make a chart of their choices, then allow time for sharing the reports.

Reading Challenge

Challenge another class to a reading contest. Set a time limit for the contest. Keep a chart on the classroom door or window to indicate number of pages or books read.

Rehearsed Reading

Help develop comprehensions skills by asking students to prepare a shore excerpt from a story to read to the class. They will need to work on expression based on content.

Schedule "performance time" into your regular reading lessons.

Reading Matchup

Ask class members and school staff to contribute samples of reading material they think is characteristic of their interests. Display them without identifying the contributors. Post a list of contributors nearby. Invite students to study the display and try to match the contributor with the reading material.

Samples might include sports magazines, mystery novels, baseball cards, play programs, travel guides, owner's manual, recipe card or horoscope clipping.

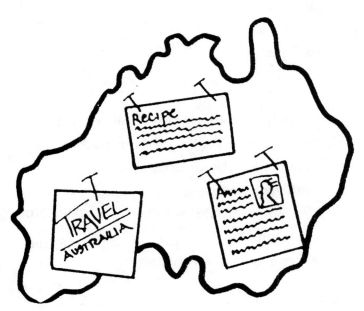

Reading Around the World

Get Global! Post a large map of the world. Keep a supply of pushpins, and yarn handy.

Search for books, magazine articles, travel brochures, recipes and news clippings about different countries. Connect the reading material or summary of material read, to the subject country with a length of yarn and pushpins .

As a variation, select a country then ask everyone to look specifically for reading material about that country. Plan some time to share and discuss the books and magazines students found.

Reading POWER

Sentence Starters

> *Read the sentence spark aloud. Encourage attentive listening by reading the sentence only two times. Give students a couple minutes to write a sentence in response. Share your sentences by inviting a student to write theirs on the board. Punctuate, capitalize and check spelling together.*

Write a sentence ...

... with three colors in it

... with nine words that tells about an animal

... that would make your friend laugh out loud

... that a three-year-old might say

... that tells someone to do something

... describing your worst habit

... telling what a pilot might say to the control tower

... that tells what a giraffe would say if it could talk

... convincing your parents to let you stay up later

... with three animal sounds in it

... about your worst fear

... that tells something great about yourself

... describing the perfect ice cream sundae

... about one of the seven dwarfs

... with your name in it

... beginning with the word *first* and ending with *last*

... describing your favorite pizza

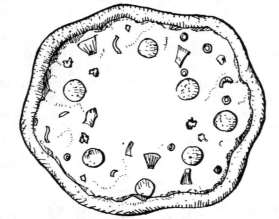

My favorite pizza has cheese and pepperoni on it.

Just for fun ...

Choose one of the sentences to illustrate. Everyone can illustrate the same one and compare the results or choose different ones and write the sentence with a caption underneath.

Liven Up Language

Perk up your days and increase parts of speech comprehension with special days. Involve students in the planning and implementing of the themes suggested below. A few ideas are included to spark your planning.

Verb Voyage ▼▼▼▼▼▼▼

- Pantomime action words.
- Head outside with a stopwatch and compare walking, hopping, crawling times for the same distance.
- Write action stories. Include at least 10 different verbs.

Adjective Adventure ▲▲▲▲▲▲▲

- Write adjective similes. "As pretty as a ..."
- Paint pictures. Start with an adjective in mind—lively, gloomy, dramatic etc.
- Start with an object. Brainstorm a list of descriptive adjectives.

Antonym Antics ▼▼▼▼▼▼▼

- Cut and paste contrast pictures.
- Come dressed with your clothes on backwards.
- Play a game of "Do the opposite". If your partner walks, you run. If your partner pretends to laugh, you cry.

Homonym Happening ▲▲▲▲▲▲▲

- Write creative stories that start with a homonym title.
  Which Witch Was It?
  Tale of a Rabbit's Tail
- Fold a sheet of paper in half. Illustrate homonym pairs, one picture in each half.
- Write homonym sentences. "I played <u>pool</u>. Then I swam in the <u>pool</u>."

Noun Events ▲▲▲▲▲▲▲

- Write sentences containing at least three *alliterative* nouns. "The <u>ship</u> had <u>shells</u> on the <u>shelves</u>.
- Each student chooses a noun to research and present in a short talk.
- Play "Name that Noun". Take turns giving clues as to the identity of a noun. Proper nouns can be included.

Math Encounters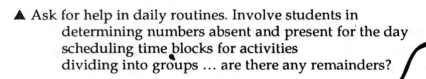

These integrated activities provide lots of hands-on learning. Working cooperatively and independently, students use manipulatives that encourage problem solving and learning a variety of math strategies.

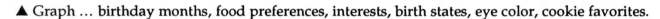

▲ Ask for help in daily routines. Involve students in
   determining numbers absent and present for the day
   scheduling time blocks for activities
   dividing into groups ... are there any remainders?

● Measure
   distance of a paper airplane flight
   roll of a marble
   a long jump

■ Practice with a directional compass. Create a treasure map.

▲ Graph ... birthday months, food preferences, interests, birth states, eye color, cookie favorites.

● Take a walk and look for geometric shapes. (tires, sun etc.)

■ Make geo-boards using nails driven into wood blocks. Provide rubber bands and shape cards for duplicating ... or create shapes on their own.

▲ Use lengths of yarn to create a variety of simple closed curves. Now head outside with a ball of yarn to create a "larger-than-life" simple closed curve!

● Use decks of cards to invent math games.

■ Read the "Guiness Book of World Records."

▲ Establish patterns while jumping rope.

● Chart the daily temperature.

■ Look in collector's journals for values of coins, stamps and trading cards. Compare values.

▲ Use string to measure the circumference of fruit. Compare the results within each fruit category.

● Set up a calculator center. Allow students to learn about more advanced math concepts.
   Learn all the key functions.
   Calculate food costs.
   Learn how to use a check ledger.
   Follow the changes of a particular stock.

Math Encounters...▲•■▲•■▲•■▲•■▲•■▲•■▲•
●▼■●▼■●▼■●▼■●▼■●▼■●▼■●▼

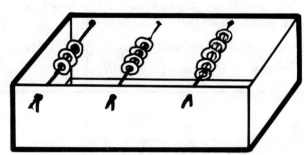

▲ Make an abacus. Make beads from self-hardening clay. Poke a hold through the center. When dry, string beads on yarn. Thread through a shoebox, as shown.

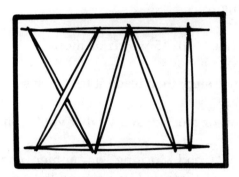

● Make individual sandboxes. Fill a giftbox with sand. Use for writing problems, computing. Smooth the sand to erase and get ready for the next number.

■ Make a toothpick chart displaying Roman numerals.

▲ Learn to count in another language.

● Challenge students to make magic squares. When added together, all the rows,—horizontal, diagonal and vertical— add up to the same number.

4	9	2
3	5	7
8	1	6

MAGIC SQUARE

■ Create combinations. Start with five buttons of different colors and two boxes. How many different combinations can be created?

▲ Glue beans on cardboard to create visual aids for square numbers.

▲ Roleplay these situations—*in metric terms!*
  • be a car owner buying gasoline
  • being a seamstress buying fabric
  • read a recipe to a friend
  • be a police officer giving a ticket for speeding
  • be a traveler and ask for directions to the nearest town
  • be a pilot and radio your altitude to the control tower
  • be a nurse and weigh a patient

Learn Something New!
Learn Something Fun!

*For a change of pace, encourage your students to learn something new **on their own** to share with the class. The learning should involve reading and research, mastering the technique, and then arranging for a "show" week when a few students each day present their newly-learned **fun** skill.*

These are some of the activities you can suggest:

👍 Learn how to juggle.

👍 Learn a tongue twister of 15 words or more.

👍 Learn a new dance step; then teach it to the class.

👍 Learn how to knit or crochet; show what you've made.

👍 Learn how to say "Good Morning" or another phrase in 4 languages: Spanish, French, German and Italian.

👍 Learn a card trick.

👍 Learn a magic trick.

👍 Learn how to draw a cartoon or create a cartoon strip.

👍 Learn how to cook or bake something new; share the recipe with the class.

👍 Learn a new art technique and share your work with the class.

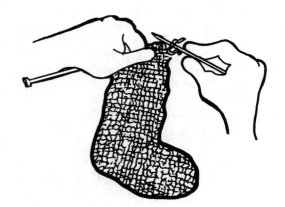

👍 Learn a new melody on a musical instrument of your choice to perform for the class.

👍 Design a new fashion outfit or costume and model it for the class.

👍 Memorize a long poem or dramatic work to recite for the class.

98

☆ CLASSROOM CONTESTS ☆

Add fun and spark up a rainy or slow day with these surprise contests.
Award a small treat or certificate of recognition to the "winning" students.

★ The student wearing the most colorful pair of socks

★ The student wearing the most buttons

★ The student wearing the most wornout blue jeans

★ The student with the most nutritious home-packed lunch

★ The student wearing the most red (or any other color)

★ The 8th student to walk through the door after lunch

★ The student who has the neatest desk at 11 AM (or any other set time)

★ A courteous and generous student

★ The student wearing the most jewelry

★ The best athlete or sport of the day

★ The most creative or artistic student of the day

★ The most helpful-to-other-students computer whiz

★ The student with the all-around best grades of the day

★ The student who shows special school spirit

★ The student with a brand new haircut

★ The first student to notice...
   ...your new hair-do (cut)
   ...something different about the classroom
   ...a new arrangement of flowers on your desk

★ The student with the most comfortable-looking shoes

★ The student who can correctly recite the words to the national anthem.

Food can provide a lot of pleasure—in more ways than you imagined! Try some of these taste-based sparks and learn about good eating habits in the process.

FOOD FUN

FOOD GROUP TALLY

Brainstorm a list of popular student dishes.
Start with
- pizza
- spaghetti and meatballs
- macaroni and cheese
- peanut butter and jelly sandwich
- tacos
- hamburger
- fish and chips
- banana split

Now consider each dish. See if you can name the food groups included in each. For example:
- **Cheeseburger**—3 groups
    bread & cereal—bun
    meat—burger patty
    fruit & vegetable—tomato, lettuce

FAVORITE SANDWICH

Ask everyone who enters ...
    "What is your favorite sandwich?"

Track the results on a classroom graph. Don't forget to ask all class members, too. Is it bologna ... ham and cheese ... tuna ... peanut butter & jelly?

Plan a special sandwich day. Get together for lunch. Everyone bring your favorite sandwich to dine on.

FOODS AROUND THE WORLD

Do people around the world eat balanced meals? Ask each pair of students to select a country and research a typical meal. Share the results.

What ingredients sound familiar? Which would you like to try? Which sound absolutely horrible? Are any meals the same that you enjoy in your own home?

Make a chart of familiar meals and their country of origin.
    For example:
    Pizza—Italy
    Taco—Mexico

PICTURE A MEAL

Start with a paper plate, magazines, scissors, and glue.

Cut out pictures of food and glue to the plate to create a balanced meal. Label all the food groups represented.

WORD SEARCH

Provide large-grid graph paper. Challenge students to create a word search of foods. First they must create a list, being sure to correctly spell each one.

After the word search is completed, trade with a classmate to find the hidden words.

E	I	P	E
M	G	E	L
D	E	G	E

DINE WITH A FRIEND

Invite guests to a balanced meal. Then plan and prepare it together in class.

If you decide to prepare breakfast, one group might be in charge of slicing bananas. Another can make toast. A third can mix hot chocolate. And a fourth can fry some sausage.

Create invitations, place mats and centerpieces that reflect the balanced meal theme.

YOU ARE WHAT YOU EAT

Everyone has heard this expression before! Now make it come to life.

Help each other trace the outline of your body on butcher paper. Use heave marker to darken the outline.

Fill your body with pictures of food cut from magazines. Glue in a collage to the body shape. Add yarn hair to crate some individuality! Hang over each student's desk.

FOOD FUN

On the FUNNY Side

If laughter is, indeed, "the best medicine", assume the role of "Doctor of the Class".

It's a Joke!

- Plan a "share-a-joke-with-your-classmates" time. Be sure to discuss appropriate jokes to tell beforehand.

- Make up "Knock-Knock" jokes.

- Identify the punch line in each joke. Discuss its importance.

- Keep a shelf of joke books handy for free time reading or share-a-joke-time preparation.

It's in the Funnies!

- Read comic books.

- Adopt a comic strip character.
  Look for ...
    - products in the store
    - specials on television
    - books about the character
  Try...
    - assuming the character's identity in a story
    - creating potential story plots for the character

- Read and discuss a comic strip together, daily.

- Make a list of comic strip authors. Write to some of them.

It's in the Laugh!

- Talk about things that make you laugh.

- Learn to laugh at yourself.

- Look for humor in everyday situations. Talk about them.

- Listen to the different ways that people laugh.

- Make a tape recording of the class laughing. Play it back. What's the reaction?

- Try to create different kinds of laughter—*giggle, chuckle, snicker, guffaw, cackle, chortle.* Include them in a story.

It's for Fun!

- Rent a comedy. Talk about the parts that were the funniest—and why.

- Plan an "everybody loves a clown" day.

Quick Crafts

> *Here are some make-it-in-a-minute ideas to set in a center for independent craft activities that keep hands constructively active and get desks and closets better organized!*

All-Purpose Container

Clean out a margarine tub—any size. Cut and apply contact paper to the bowl. Glue a sample of the item to be stored inside to the lid. Some good candidates are: paper clips, crayons, markers

Pencil Holders

- Clean out empty juice cans. Cover with pieces of masking tape. Paint.
- Use self-hardening clay. Shape the clay into a dome—flat on the bottom, rounded top. The rounded top must be about 2 inches (5 cm) deep.
  Use the end of an unsharpened pencil to make several holes in the clay. Test the pencil to be sure it will stand in the hole by itself. When hardened, paint the dome to resemble a turtle, ladybug or other animal/insect.

Yarn Dispenser

Decorate a 4-inch square (12 cm)—or approximate size box—with lengths of colorful yarn. Poke a hole in the lid. Place a ball of string, yarn or ribbon inside the box. Thread one end through the hole in the lid. Put the lid on. No more tangles in art cabinets or drawers!

Memo Holder

Start with a 2-inch (5 cm) square tile. Decorate using cotton-tipped swabs dipped in tempera paint.
Use tacky glue to attach a wooden clothespin to the back at the center of the tile. Make sure the "wide open" end of the clothespin is even with the bottom edge of the tile.
Write memos on index cards and clip to the memo holder for easy-to-see reminders.

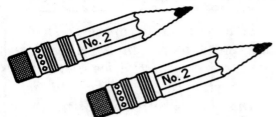

& Stencils

Save this activity for a rainy day when recess is out of the question.

Have on hand a wide selection of stencil and colored pencils. Invite students to use these tools to create original artwork.

Toy stores sell a variety of inexpensive plastic stencils that are long lasting and will be an asset to your permanent art supply collection. The variety of stencils should include:

- upper and lowercase letters
- numerals
- symbols
- animals
- flowers
- geometric shapes
- holiday designs

With pencils and stencils, students can try their hand at creating:

- greeting card messages
- bulletin board borders
- decorative book covers
- book report covers
- note cards for personalized writing
- bulletin board lettering
- wall borders
- name plaques
- spelling word designs
- name initial designs

After the stencil outline ha been traced with pencil, students may use bold or fine-line, bright colored markers to re-outline the pattern for greater visual impact.

Encourage students to design their own stencils from lightweight tag board. A wide selection of stencils will bring many pleasurable hours of innovative art to the classroom.

The Sound of Music

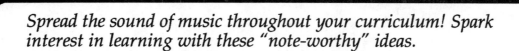

Spread the sound of music throughout your curriculum! Spark interest in learning with these "note-worthy" ideas.

Set the mood with music. Play background music for a variety of classroom activities. Involve students in selecting music appropriate to the situation. For example, classical music might accompany sustained silent reading. Clean up time might need a boost with a current popular tune.

Listen to and learn to identify different types of music—
jazz, country, pop, classical, opera, hymns, folk

Make your own musical instruments. Try oatmeal box bongos, shoe box string instruments.

Start a Kazoo Club or Harmonious Harmonica Group. Listen to tones. Learn to play a tune.

Find out about the different kinds of instruments—woodwind, brass, percussion, string, keyboard.

Research unusual instruments—bagpipes, accordion, harpsichord, chimes, castanets, tambourine.

Write sentences and memorize spelling to popular or familiar music.

Illustrate song lyrics.

Learn to dance! Waltz, tango, folk and square dance your way through physical education.

Estimate how many keys are on a piano keyboard. Count and determine the closest guess.

Invite the owner of a music store to visit and talk about his or her business.

Read sheet music. Are there any familiar elements? How does it compare to regular reading? What elements do they share?

Roleplay the part of a conductor leading an orchestra.

Make a list of interesting facts about famous composers.

DRESS-UP Days

Every now and then a class needs a pick-me-up—something to rekindle the zest for school. When you sense that your group needs a fun change, try one of these special dress-up days.

Give student's a couple days notice and ask that they wear ...

- only black and white
- jeans and a t-shirt (with writing on it)
- a top and bottom with mis-matched patterns
- two different socks and two different shoes
- an unusual hat
- an outfit with no buttons
- a striped shirt–vertical or horizontal
- a favorite outfit
- a checkered or plaid shirt, skirt, blouse or pants
- only red, white and blue
- in a specific color
- clothing to coordinate with a holiday
- something resembling an animal—stripes, spots, etc.
- everything backwards
- career clothing
- a sports uniform
- something a character in a story you're reading might wear
- a necktie or scarf
- clothing from another country
- something resembling a fruit or vegetable
- a sweatshirt or t-shirt with from another city or state

Natural Fun

Learning in the great outdoors . . .

Take a Hike

Take a color walk. . .assign groups different colors to look for
Hunt High and Low . . Make lists of things higher and lower than your head
Litter Lookers . . . Keep track of how much litter you see—and can pick up
Natural or Man-made . . . List things produced by nature or man
Directionals . . . Call out directions for the group to follow
Larger-than-life . . . Arm yourselves with magnifying glasses

Collectors

Individual or group collections lead to reading, sharing and research.

butterflies	rocks
leaves	dried flowers
feathers	nuts
cactus	plants

Nature . . . in General

Find out about as many insects as you can.
Have a pebble tossing contest . . . measure the results.
Collect some twigs and create imaginary animals.
Start a birdwatching club
Make a classroom leaf chart.
Write a story from the viewpoint of an ant.
Plant some bulbs for spring bloom.
Conduct soil testing experiments
Build a snowman with a predetermined diameter.

START A CLASS CLUB!

Here's an opportunity to enrich student learning while working cooperatively with other teachers in your school. Create "clubs" for students utilizing the best and individual talents of each teacher.

GETTING STARTED:

Meet with all interested teachers. Discuss your talents, hobbies, and special interests. Once it has been determined what club each teacher will lead, the concept is easy: Set aside a specific time period weekly or bi-weekly for students to attend the club of their choice. All students are given a list of club choices and their scheduled meetings. Ask students to list their first choice plus two alternates. Space is filled on a first come/first serve basis with a specific limit in group size.

CLUB TIPS:

● Group students by grade levels for club choices... K-2, 3-4, 5-6 or K-1, 2-3, 4-5 depending on grade levels in your school and student enrollment.

● Be sure that time and meeting locations are made clear to the students. You may want to consider offering clubs to certain grade levels only such a grades 4,5,6. It is important that all students in the grade participate so that the enrichment opportunity is open to all students. Clubs should be for enrichment and teach beyond the regular curriculum.

● The clubs can be as informal or as structured as the teachers choose. It is important, however, that students depend on a specific time period for their club to meet and that this extra-curricular enrichment be an activity that students and teachers look forward to and enjoy on a regular basis— whether it is weekly or bi-weekly.

● Let students participate in a "catchy" name for their club. Consider these club focus and names:

  ● Musical instruments—The Jammers
  ● Cars—Hot Rodders
  ● Rockets & Planets—Space Cadettes
  ● Gardening—Green Thumbs

CLASS CLUBS

Why not meet with interested teachers soon and brainstorm "Class Clubs" for your school?
Here are some club suggestions to get you started!

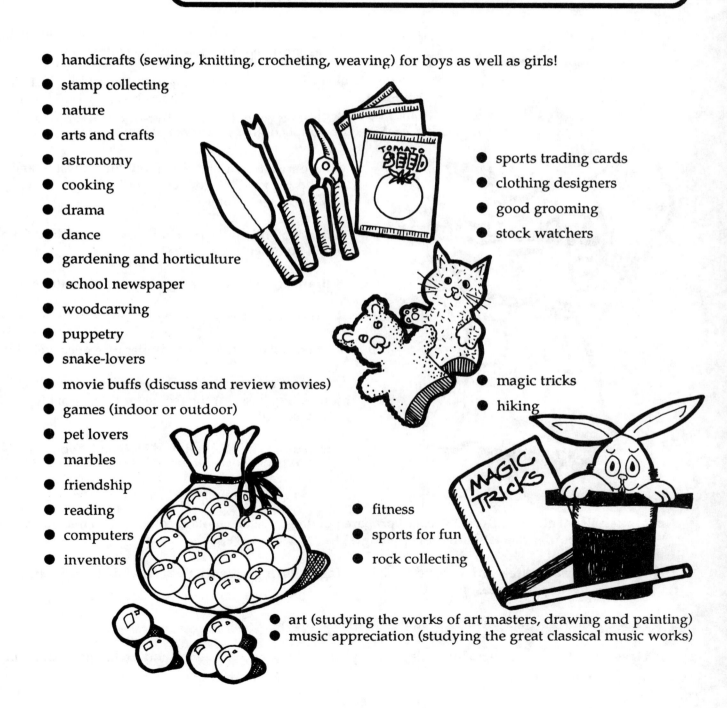

- handicrafts (sewing, knitting, crocheting, weaving) for boys as well as girls!
- stamp collecting
- nature
- arts and crafts
- astronomy
- cooking
- drama
- dance
- gardening and horticulture
- school newspaper
- woodcarving
- puppetry
- snake-lovers
- movie buffs (discuss and review movies)
- games (indoor or outdoor)
- pet lovers
- marbles
- friendship
- reading
- computers
- inventors

- sports trading cards
- clothing designers
- good grooming
- stock watchers

- magic tricks
- hiking

- fitness
- sports for fun
- rock collecting

- art (studying the works of art masters, drawing and painting)
- music appreciation (studying the great classical music works)

> *Develop delicious curriculum delights with these ideas for fun with food!*

What's Cookin'?

- **Make** and sell a class cookbook with a collection of cookie recipes.

- **Prepare** a seasonal feast with 4-5 groups each being responsible for preparing one course.

- **Enjoy** a selection of unusual berries in the fall.

- **Start** off each day with a nutritious treat for a week's time.

- **Prepare** a nutritious 'fast food' lunch; test it; and send the ideas off to McDonald's, Burger King, Wendy's, etc. for a response.

- **Make** a bulletin board of creative cold drinks for a hot summer day.

- **Brainstorm** new cooking ideas for plain toast.

- **Create** new uses for honey.

- **Make** a list of foods that applesauce goes well with.

- **Prepare** and serve refreshments for the next faculty meeting. Pass out the recipe for the special food you served.

- **Discuss:** When is food 'fun'? When is food 'not fun'?

- **Make** a list of all the different ways to prepare potatoes. Create a potato collage from magazines and labels and border the list with these photographs.

- **Prepare** a class-made soup with students bringing in the ingredients. (Try vegetable soup, fruit soup, bean soup, or a seasonal soup.)

- **Plan** an indoor winter picnic. Let students create a theme.

- **Have** a sandwich exchange lunch day—every student brings a sandwich and exchanges half or all of it with another student.

Now that food is on your mind, here are some more tasty, multicurricular ideas.

Food for Thought

🍰 **Compile** a category cookbook—all desserts, all appetizers or main dishes.

🍰 **Make a list** of foods with double letters. (carrot, lettuce, beef) Whose list is the longest? Combine lists to create a class list and invite students to continue to add to it as they discover new foods during the course of other reading and writing activities.

🍰 **Locate** some "no-cooking" recipes, that require only mixing, blending cutting, etc. Prepare a chosen recipe for parents and guests to enjoy during Back-to-School night or Open House.

🍰 **Make class graphs** of favorites: fruits, ice cream flavors, fun foods, restaurants

🍰 **Look for** some international recipes. Compare the ingredients to those in foods favored by students. Any similarities? What are the differences? Bring some of the unusual spices to class to sniff and examine.

🍰 **Discover** foods and recipes that are common to many countries but have different names.

🍰 **Find** foods that are eaten only in your or originated in your country.

🍰 **Write** food riddles.

What is long, yellow and is a-peeling? — *a banana*

🍰 **Pretend** that birthday cakes were never invented. Make an art project that pictures the substitute treat.

🍰 **Set up** a literature corner filled with stories based on food. Some suggestions are: *Blueberries for Sal, How Pizza Came to Queens, Frannie's Fruits, Sam's Sandwich.*

🍰 **Research** the origin of food and food names. How did the *hot dog* come to be? Why is *pizza* called a pie? Who created *doughnuts*?

Open-Ended ART

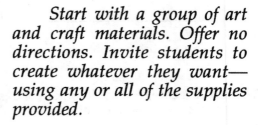

Start with a group of art and craft materials. Offer no directions. Invite students to create whatever they want— using any or all of the supplies provided.

Group One

- ◆ watercolor paints
- ◆ paper plates
- ◆ cotton balls
- ◆ paste
- ◆ glitter

Group Two

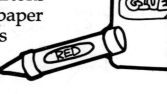

- ◆ milk cartons
- ◆ tissue paper
- ◆ crayons
- ◆ glue
- ◆ yarn

Group Three

- ◆ construction paper
- ◆ colored pencils
- ◆ masking tape
- ◆ empty cans
- ◆ scissors

Group Four

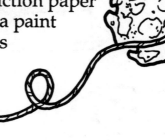

- ◆ construction paper
- ◆ tempera paint
- ◆ sponges
- ◆ straws
- ◆ string

Group Five

◆ popsicle sticks
◆ butcher paper
◆ macaroni
◆ felt pens
◆ lace

Group Six

◆ fabric scraps
◆ paper tubes
◆ newspaper
◆ glue
◆ clay

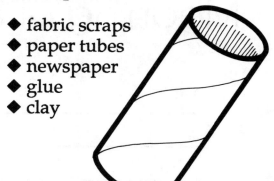

Group Seven

◆ aluminum foil
◆ ribbon/bows
◆ muffin cups
◆ clothespins
◆ giftwrap

Group Eight

◆ sequins & buttons
◆ tempera paint
◆ paper cups
◆ toothpicks
◆ paste

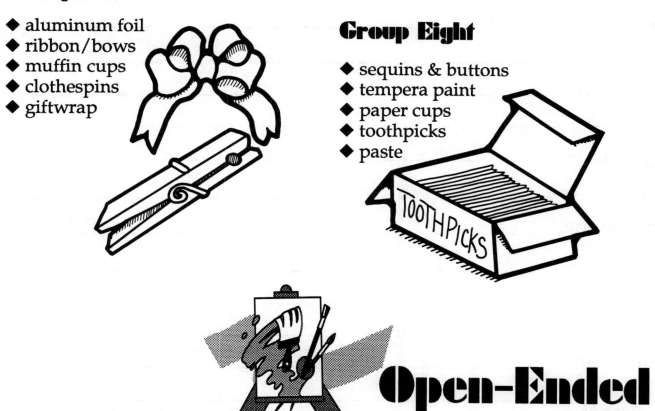

TOOTHPICKS

Open-Ended ART

Seatwork Jump Start

Did you know that you spend about 1200 hours in school each year?

The TRUE Meaning of School

Look up these "school" words in the dictionary. Write their TRUE meaning (definition) next to it. Then use the word in a sentence that shows the meaning.

cafeteria _____

_____

library _____

_____

encyclopedia _____

_____

atlas _____

_____

dictionary _____

_____

gymnasium _____

_____

auditorium _____

_____

teacher _____

_____

computer _____

_____

globe _____

_____

About Me

Share some information about yourself.

Something I do well _____

Something I would like to learn to do _____

My favorite game or sport _____

What I like to collect _____

My favorite pet or animal _____

What makes me smile _____

Someone I admire _____

What I enjoy doing most _____

A famous person I would like to meet _____

My favorite food _____

A very special friend or relative _____

My best quality _____

Something about me you would be surprised to know

_____

Sports
Shorts

Write a short description of each sport. Then read a description to a classmate and find out if he or she can name the sport by listening to the description you wrote.

Think about equipment, players, rules and scoring.

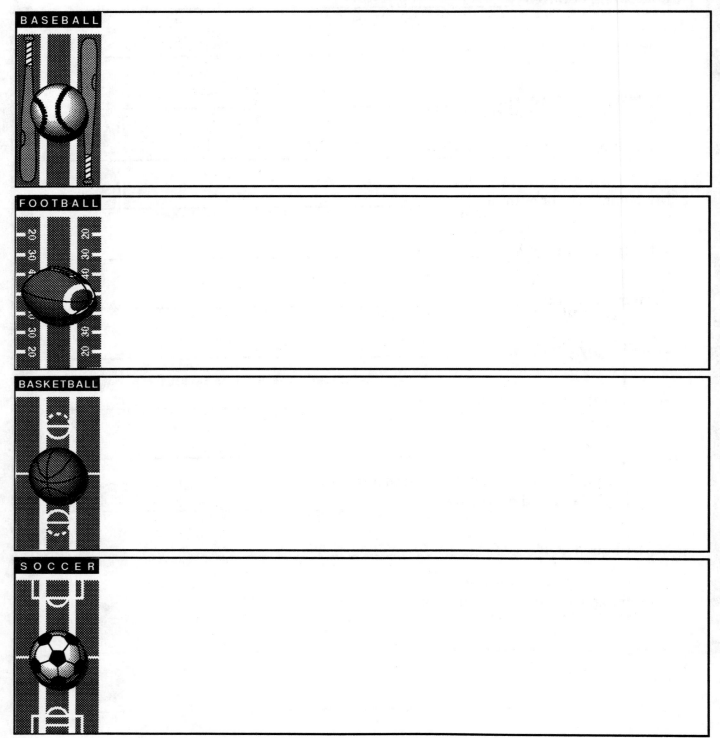

BASEBALL

FOOTBALL

BASKETBALL

SOCCER

Multicurricular SPRINGBOARDS & STARTERS © EDUPRESS

Animal Fact

Travel the world to hunt down some amazing facts about animals in encyclopedias or animal books.
Write your answers on another piece of paper. Find at least eight.

Safari

1. What is in a camel's hump?

2. How much does an adult rhinoceros weigh?

3. How does a baby kangaroo travel?

4. How many pounds (kg) of food does an African elephant eat in a day?

5. What is an elephant's tusk made of?

6. What is the only food a Koala will eat?

7. How fast can a cheetah run?

8. What is the only mammal that can fly?

9. Why does a zebra have stripes?

10. How big are hippopotamus' teeth?

11. What does a porcupine use for protection?

12. What is the only animal that can really laugh?

13. How can a yak survive in cold temperatures?

14. How long is an anteater's tongue?

15. How does a beaver build its home?

16. How does a monkey use its tail?

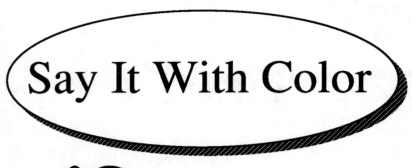

Say It With Color

There are lots of ways to say things.

Think about color, for example. Picture "powder blue" in your mind. Now picture "dark blue". Are they the same? Probably not.

Look through catalogs, magazines and books to find other words to describe color. Write them in the box below each color word.

Here are some examples to get you started. What about <u>watermelon</u> <u>red</u>, <u>sunshine</u> <u>yellow</u> or <u>cinnamon</u> <u>brown</u>?

RED	**YELLOW**	**BLUE**

ORANGE	**GREEN**	**BROWN**

Words that Describe

Which is easier to picture in your mind?
  a hamburger… or a **thick, juicy** hamburger?
  a bike … or a **shiny, new** bike?

Words can make things "come to life". Think of words to describe the things below. Write them under the word. Share your list with your classmates. Put together one big list for each thing. How many words did you think of?

pie

1. _____
2. _____
3. _____
4. _____
5. _____
6. _____

ocean

1. _____
2. _____
3. _____
4. _____
5. _____
6. _____

butterfly

1. _____
2. _____
3. _____
4. _____
5. _____
6. _____

necklace

1. _____
2. _____
3. _____
4. _____
5. _____
6. _____

ice cream

1. _____
2. _____
3. _____
4. _____
5. _____
6. _____

cloud

1. _____
2. _____
3. _____
4. _____
5. _____
6. _____

Put-togethers

Examples:

A woman was crying because her window was broken.

I met a friend to play and then we ate a hot dog.

Directions:

Put together a sentence.

*Use a phrase from **column 1** and a phrase from **column 2**. Add as many other words as you want. Change the phrases a little if you need to.*

How many different sentences can you make? You may need more paper.

Look at the examples for ideas.

1.

car ran out of gas
forgot my homework
house is for sale
window was broken
met a friend to play
ran across the street
talked to a teacher
wanted to forget it
shared her lunch
walked my dog

2.

a woman was crying
met a new friend
lost the key
got caught in the rain
ate a hot dog
drove to the store
went on a trip
had dinner late
went outside to meet her
cooked a big dinner

Give an Example

> *Try to give an example when you are talking to others. It helps them to understand what you mean. Practice that skill. Give an example for each thing listed below.*

• a bad habit _____

• something with fur _____

• a form of transportation _____

• an irritating sound _____

• a snack food _____

• a good quality in a friend _____

• a bad quality in a friend _____

• somewhere you would find a crowd _____

• a good idea _____

• something sharp _____

• a sour fruit _____

• a helpful thing to do _____

• a flying insect _____

• something cold _____

• something hot _____

• something difficult to do _____

SANDWICH CHEF

Become a chef and create a new kind of sandwich.
Write all the information in the slice of bread below.
Turn the paper over and draw a picture of your creation.
Look in the box for some hints about the information.

NAME—Give your sandwich a name—*Bologna Surprise, Salami Sunrise, Cheese Stack*
KIND OF BREAD—sliced, roll, bun? Rye, wheat, raisin?
INGREDIENTS—meat, cheese, fruit, lettuce?
CONDIMENTS—mustard, jelly, mayonnaise?
SPECIAL INSTRUCTIONS—top with an olive, stack in a special order?

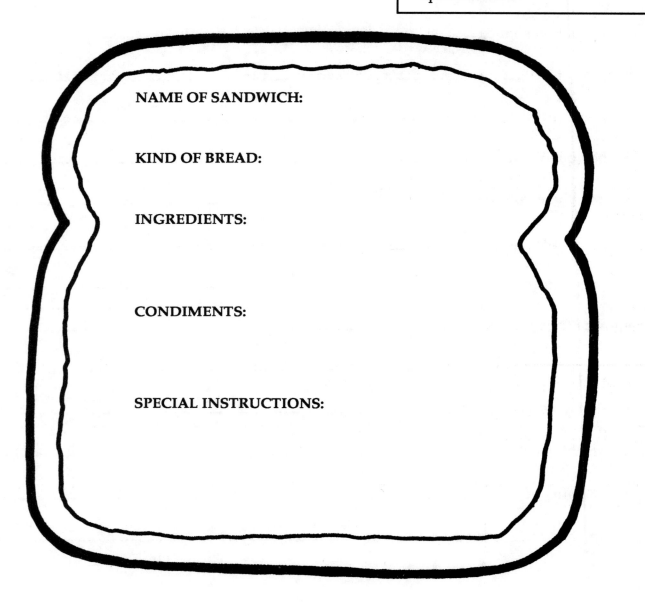

NAME OF SANDWICH:

KIND OF BREAD:

INGREDIENTS:

CONDIMENTS:

SPECIAL INSTRUCTIONS:

Homonym Pairs

*Look at each pair of words. They are **homonymns**. They sound the same but their meanings are different. Write a sentence for each word pair. Be sure the sentence includes both words and that their meanings are clear.*

Turn your paper over and illustrate three of them.

guest — guessed

_____

foul — fowl

_____

for — four

_____

beet — beat

_____

piece — peace

_____

right — write

_____

bear — bare

_____

presents — presence

_____

kernel — colonel

_____

strait — straight

_____

blue — blew

_____

"Direct Quotes"

Spark a lesson in using quotation marks and build a bulletin board at the same time!

Suggestions for subjects are on these two pages. All you do is gather what is suggested, follow the guidelines for obtaining student quotes, then create a simple display.

Quotes from Student Stars

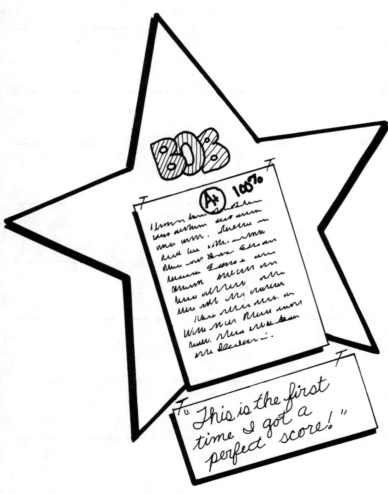

Every Monday morning place five names on the bulletin board. Invite those children to select something to display from their previous week's papers . You might want to warn them in advance that their name will appear the following week.

Ask the student stars to write an accompanying quote. For example, if a student decides to post a spelling paper he might write

"This is the first time I got a perfect score!"

Or if a student decides to display a work of art she might write,

"I love the colors in this painting!"

Be sure to check for accurate punctuation and placement of quotation marks.

Encourage classmates to write a direct quote to each student on display, remarking on their efforts. Again, stress correct quotation usage.

Cut a large star to back each student's achievement.

Clear the board on Friday and get ready for a new group of starts o Monday.

"Direct Quotes"

Quotes from our Families

"I hate how my hair looks in this picture!"

Ask students to bring a picture of a family member—sibling, parent, grandparent, aunt, uncle or cousin. Have them obtain a direct quote from that family member. For example, a student's brother might say,

"I hate how my hair looks in this picture!"

Or a student might write their own quote about the family member in the picture. For example, if he or she decides to post a picture of a sister the quote might read,

"Sometimes my sister bugs me but I like when we play soccer together."

Quotes About our Homes

"I love our apple tree in the spring."

Ask students to bring a photo that features their home. It might be an outdoor shot or a photo of one of the rooms.

Again, request a quote to display along with the photograph.

If the picture features the kitchen, the quote might read,

"I love how the kitchen smells when my mom is busy cooking."

Maybe the photo features the student's bedroom. The quote might read,

"I cleaned my room for this picture. It may never be clean again!"

Bulletin Board Boosts

Make a bulletin board a vocabulary-building center. Cut tag board into flashcard-type strips. Select from the suggestions below. Write the words in colorful marking pen on the tag board then follow the directions for each suggestion.

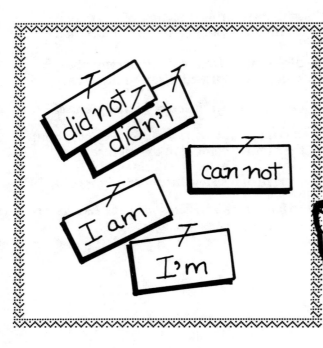

MATCH UPS

Create two sets of words. Keep one set in a basket next to the bulletin board. Put extra push-pins on the board. Look at the word on the board, select a match in the basket, then pin the match to the bulletin board.

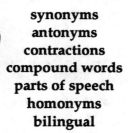

synonyms
antonyms
contractions
compound words
parts of speech
homonyms
bilingual

ORDERING

Create one set of words. Tack them in random order on the bulletin board. Leave an empty column to the left or right of the words. Retack the words in order, top to bottom, in the empty column.

alphabetical
size words
number of vowels

INTERACTION

• Post **verbs.** Select and pantomime.

• Relocate randomly placed words to make a sentence.

CATEGORICALLY SPEAKING

Divide a strip of butcher paper into three sections. At the top of each section, boldly print a heading. Look at the categories below for suggestions.

Provide a stack of donated magazines scissors and glue. Invite students to clip pictures they think fit a heading then glue the picture in the matching section on the butcher paper. Take time to discuss their decisions.

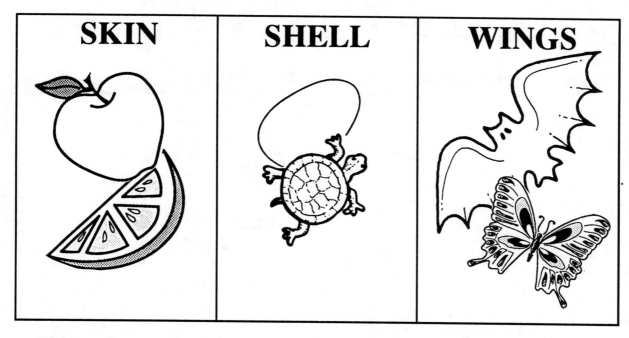

SKIN   **SHELL**   **WINGS**

Things that are found
- land, sea, air
- jungle, desert, mountains
- indoors, outdoors, both

Things that can
- fly, swim, walk
- jump, crawl, dig
- push, pull, lift

Things that are
- sweet, sour, spicy
- safe, dangerous, scary
- short, tall, wide

Things that have
- wheels, buttons, motors
- skin, shells, horns
- roots, tails, wings

Things that make you
- laugh, cry, sigh
- cough, sneeze, get goosebumps
- tired, relaxed, energetic

Things that feel
- hot, cold, slimy
- soft, rough, squishy
- heavy, light, fluffy

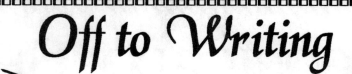

Off to Writing

Collect a variety of hats to tack to the bulletin board. All sorts of can be found inexpensively at a local thrift shop. Students can contribute, too.

Leave room underneath each hat for student writing projects. Choose a hat, then write

- a creative story
- a sentence describing the hat
- a paragraph about someone who might have worn the hat

Hats can also be removed and worn on for some impromptu roleplaying or storytelling.

Assembly Required

This bulletin board involves students in learning and directionality.

Provide paper parts for the suggested items below. Label them or make the board even more challenging by asking students to match a label to a part.

Provide the parts in a box along with pushpins. Once assembled, the student takes the parts apart and returns them to the box for the next assembler.

Skeleton
... human or otherwise

Plant

Heart

Solar System
... in relation to the sun

Map of the country
... states or provinces in position

Engine

Microscope

Flag
...from your own or any other country

Rocket ship

Place setting
...pretend it's a seven-course meal!

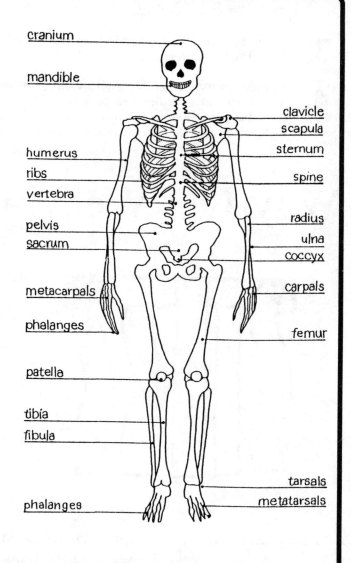

This interactive bulletin board opens the door to learning about other cultures and the variety of ways the skill of weaving is used. Plus you'll have a colorfully woven classroom wall as the result!

I. Start by cutting strips of construction paper, gift wrap or wallpaper of equal length in a variety of colors and designs. You can vary the cutting by making some strips wavy and others straight-edged.

2. Next, staple groups of strips in clusters either horizontally or vertically. Staple only the ends. Allow some slack so that children can weave paper through.

3. Place the remaining strips in a woven basket next to the bulletin board.

4. Finally, show students how to weave the strips in and out through the paper "strands" on the bulletin board. Encourage them to think of color and design as they weave.

Way-Out Weaving

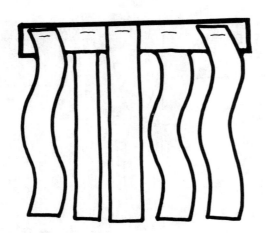

As an extra attraction, work together to create a display of baskets, blankets and other woven materials.

LINE DESIGN

Ask for contributions of leftover yarn from home knitting and craft projects. Offer students one or both of the variations below. Store the yarn, scissors and stapler or tape in a basket near the bulletin board.

OPTION ONE

- Attach the first length of yarn to the bulletin board. Students create various sized angles by cutting lengths of yarn and stapling or taping it as an extension from an existing line.
- Ask students to keep an accurate update of the triangle count.
- Encourage older students to use a protractor to measure the sizes of the angles. Discuss the term *perpendicular*. Identify perpendicular lines in the design.

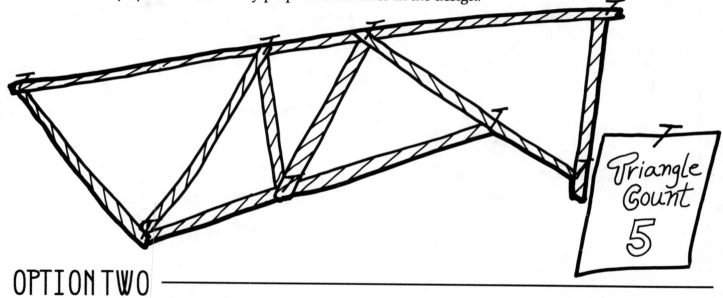

Triangle Count 5

OPTION TWO

- Cut construction paper circles and staple or tape them at random spots on the board.
- Students measure distance between two circles of their choice and cut yarn to match the measurement. Staple yarn length beginning and ending at the chosen circles.

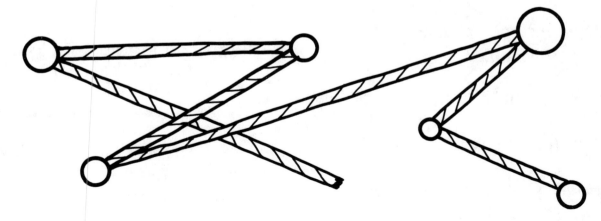

A Phrase for a Start ...
... A Finish with Art

Start with a phrase—a smilie, proverb, Murphy's Law or familiar saying. Ask children to repond to the phrase with original artwork.

Stock a table with a variety of art supplies and let creativity—and interpretation—run free. Display all artwork around the phrase.

What goes up must come down!

Here are some phrases to get you started:

Don't count your chickens before they hatch.

A bird in the hand is worth two in the bush.

Life is just a bowl of cherries.

A picture is worth a thousand words.

EVERY CLOUD HAS A SILVER LINING.

You can't teach an old dog new tricks...

Let a smile be your umbrella.

As pretty as a ...	As silly as a ...
As happy as a ...	As sharp as a ...
As quiet as a ...	As big as a ...

A Prop for a Start ...
... A Finish with Art

Start with a familar shape cut from colorful construction paper or other material. Ask children to do something specific as suggested below ... but allow it to be an original design.

Stock a table with a variety of art supplies and let imaginations— and creativity— run free. Display all artwork in or around the prop.

Here are some props to get you started:

Cut a "ceramic" vase ...
    fill it with colorful flowers

Erect a huge circus tent...
    occupy it with creative clowns

Construct an oval racetrack...
    design cars of the future

Bake a giant ice cream cone . . .
    scoop up imaginative ice cream

Build a sturdy red barn . . .
    stock the barnyard with animals

Create a large bowl...
    fill it with fresh fruit

Open up a treasure chest ...
    show what was found inside

MOST VALUABLE MEMBER

You have been
voted the most valuable
member
by the other
members in the group.

Congratulations!

TO:

GROUP MEMBERS:

Follow the directions to make make movable signs to place on student desks for motivating and rewarding.

TO MAKE ONE SIGN:

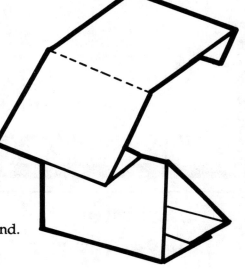

1. Cut a 12 inch (30 cm) square piece of tag board. Choose from the messages below or create your own. Write the message in bold, colorful marking pen.

2. Laminate or cover with clear contact paper.

3. Fold in half. Fold each end in one inch (2.54 cm)

4. Glue folded flaps together so that sign will stand.

Expert Speller
Math Marvel
Sparkling Student
Creative Mind
Super Problem Solver
Awesome Athlete
Writing Whiz
Marvelous Scientist
Outstanding Reader
Author of the Day

NIFTY NOTES

from your teacher

Here are some notes to photocopy, cut apart and give to students. This page has pre-written messages. Blank notes on which to create your own message are on the following page. Take your pick—then pick up a student's spirits.

Here's the Scoop …

I think you're Great!

I know you'll
do
your best
today.

Thanks for the
great idea!

MEMO

Thank You

**I think you're doing a
super job!**

Cheer UP!
Today will be better.

No bones
about it.

You're
really
trying.

NIFTY NOTES from your teacher

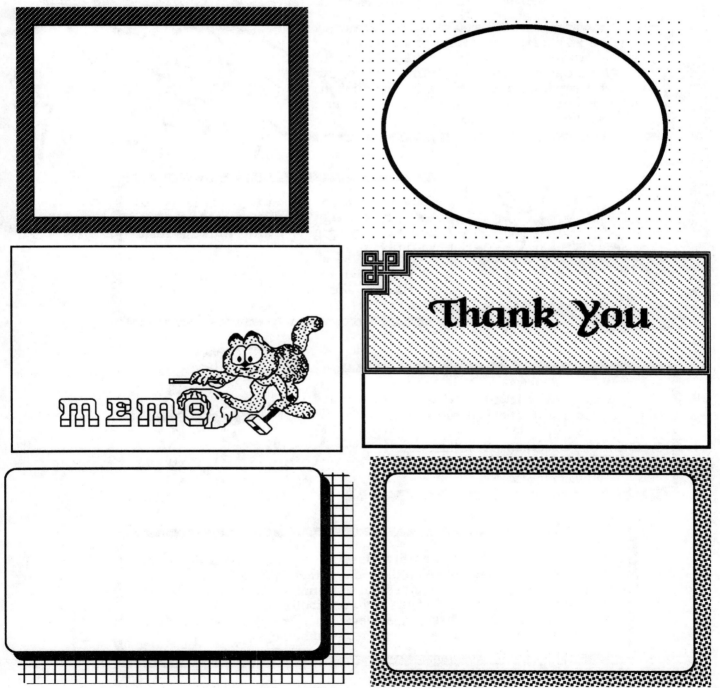

SPARK Some Smiles

What to do when you've tired of the usual methods of stars and certificates? Try these surefire ways to get students smiling at their own accomplishments.

Have 3-4 blue **ribbon awards** on hand for very special occasions. Students wear the ribbon with pride for a day or week then return it for use by another deserving student. Allow the Blue Ribbon student to be seen by the office staff, other teachers and students and the principal.

Buy inexpensive ribbon to make **fancy hair bows** . Attach a sign of achievement to the bow. Adorn a deserving girl's hairdo with the unique reward ribbon.

Attach a sign of achievement to the bill of a **baseball cap**. Offer this to the boys—for to who girl who prefers it to a hair bow!

Use large **pin-backed buttons** where the message can be changed easily. Some message ideas include:
"My math is magnificent!"
"I read five books this month!"
"Author of the week!"

Write a weekly or monthly **class newspaper.** Include special columns such as students who did well on their spelling test, students who showed great improvement in reading, students with perfect attendance, star athletes, students who contributed in a special way. List their name and contribution or achievement. Be sure all students are named in the newsletter. Make copies to send home.

SPARK Some Smiles

Create and laminate an **assortment of coupons** (see following two pages) to hand out for special jobs well done. Write the student's name using a wax pencil. The student redeems the coupon and claims a specific reward.

- Eating lunch with the teacher
- Free homework assignment
- Sit next to your friend today
- First in line all day today

Redeemed coupons are turned in, wiped clean and saved for the next deserving recipient.

Create a **video** with the students as the stars. Feature students with special accomplishments, students at work on projects in the classroom, students at free play or physical education, students making oral presentations and committees working cooperatively.

Allow students the opportunity to check out the video to take home for viewing.

Contact the local newspaper and request a reporter and photographer to come to your school or class to **publicize** special activities and students. They will feel extra pride upon seeing their names and photos in print; Plus they can clip the articles for a personal or classroom scrapbook or a special letter to friends and relatives.

Clip a Coupon

Sit
NEXT
to Your Friend
Today

Name:

Eat Lunch

with your Teacher

Name:

FREE
Homework Assignment

Name:

First in line

Name:

all day Today

Clip a Coupon

BREAKFAST
with your
Teacher

Name:

Turn In For a Treat

Name:

Good for
ONE CHOICE

From the
GOODIE GRABBAG

Name:

Name:

Cash in for Cash

Spend your "play" money at the classroom store.

Reading Challenges

Reproduce, then cut apart these reading challenges to have on hand for reading motivation.

On the first page there are book marks. Each day the student records the number of pages read. At the end of the week, total the pages.

On the next page are reading records for each book and the number of pages read. Encourage students to set their own page count goals then challenge them to reach

DAY	PAGES READ
Sunday	
Monday	
Tuesday	
Wednesday	
Thursday	
Friday	
Saturday	
TOTAL	

DAY	PAGES READ
Sunday	
Monday	
Tuesday	
Wednesday	
Thursday	
Friday	
Saturday	
TOTAL	

DAY	PAGES READ
Sunday	
Monday	
Tuesday	
Wednesday	
Thursday	
Friday	
Saturday	
TOTAL	

DAY	PAGES READ
Sunday	
Monday	
Tuesday	
Wednesday	
Thursday	
Friday	
Saturday	
TOTAL	

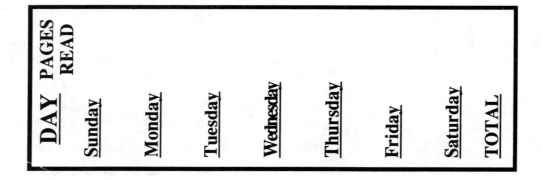

DAY	PAGES READ	Sunday	Monday	Tuesday	Wednesday	Thursday	Friday	Saturday	TOTAL

Book Title	Author	Page Count
1.		
2.		
3.		
4.		
5.		

Page Goal_____   Page Total _____

Book Title	Author	Page Count
1.		
2.		
3.		
4.		
5.		

Page Goal_____   Page Total _____

More Exciting Titles from Edupress

102 Indian Activity Book
Art•Crafts•Cooking

126 Colonial Activities
Art•Crafts•Cooking

138 Frontier Activities
Art•Crafts•Cooking

128 Easy Book Projects
Report, explore, share

134 Holiday Games
Fun-filled learning

135 Center Games
Ten easy game centers

136 Outdoor Games
Group and skill games

137 Desktop Games
Indoor learning games

140 Classroom Kickoff
Year-long resource

139 Super Arts & Crafts
Over 700 art activites

134 Oodles of Writing
Hundreds of prompts

127 Report Roundup
Research & report forms

130 Fall Projects
Multicurricular learning

131 Winter Projects
Loads of winter activities

132 Spring Projects
Apr/May/June fun

117 Wonders of Mystery
Theme units